WAR PLAN RED

WAR PLAN RED

The United States' Secret Plan to Invade Canada and Canada's Secret Plan to Invade The United States

KEVIN LIPPERT

Princeton Architectural Press · New York

Published by
Princeton Architectural Press
37 East Seventh Street
New York, New York 10003

Visit our website at www.papress.com.

Editor: Tom Cho
Designer: Mia Johnson

Special thanks to: Nicola Brower, Janet Behning,
Erin Cain, Megan Carey, Carina Cha, Andrea Chlad,
Barbara Darko, Benjamin English, Jan Cigliano Hartman,
Jan Haux, Diane Levinson, Jennifer Lippert,
Jaime Nelson, Rob Shaeffer, Sara Stemen, Marielle Suba,
Kaymar Thomas, Paul Wagner, Joseph Weston,
and Janet Wong of Princeton Architectural Press
—Kevin C. Lippert, publisher

Library of Congress Cataloging-in-Publication Data is
available from the publisher upon request

Table of Contents

INDEX TO CHAPTER XXXX

DEFENCE SCHEME NO. 1

Introduction

This book came about following a conversation with Paddy Laidley of Raincoast Books, in Vancouver, who said that Canadians are often (or was it sometimes?) interested in what their neighbors to the south think of them. I remembered her comment when, two days later, President Barack Obama assured a questioner at a press conference that the United States has no plans to invade Canada, and what better exemplifies our lack of interest than the absence of an invasion plan? (We liked Iraq enough to invade.)

The reporter's question was partly an echo of a secret document, dating back to the 1930s but declassified in 1974, outlining America's plan to invade Canada—War Plan Red—which sowed the seeds for speculation, mostly comic, about a US takeover in movies like *Canadian Bacon* and an episode of the TV show *The West Wing*. As with so many things, the States was behind Canada in thinking about neighborly takeovers: it turned out that Canada had drawn up its own invasion plan, Defence Scheme No. 1, ten years earlier. This small book offers a quick overview of these two plans, starting with a brief history of US-Canada border skirmishes.

PART ONE

THE WAR OF 1812

AN IMAGINARY LINE THROUGH THE WOODS

The British should never have lost the Revolutionary War. The Redcoats were much better armed, more disciplined, and far greater in number, surely the most powerful and feared army in the world at the time. They were not prepared, however, to fight a long war of attrition, had trouble supplying an overseas army three thousand miles away, and were caught off guard when France, one of the world's other superpowers, entered the war against them, making this an early version of Britain's Vietnam. These factors and others led to their final defeat at Yorktown, Virginia, where British commander Lord Cornwallis was outfoxed by George Washington and French general Comte de Rochambeau, and forced to surrender along with his eight thousand troops, the final straw in an increasingly unpopular and costly war back home.

Fig.1: Lord Cornwallis surrenders to George Washington
at Yorktown, October 19, 1781

What would it take to sign a peace accord, British negotiators, led by Lord Buckingham and David Hartley, asked at the treaty table in April 1782 in Paris, at the ironically named Hotel d'York? The Americans, including Benjamin Franklin, John Adams, John Jay, American ambassador Henry Laurens, and Franklin's grandson William (as secretary), had an idea: how about all of British North America (the Thirteen Colonies plus Québec, St. Johns, Newfoundland, Rupert's Land, Prince Edward Island, and Nova Scotia)? If this was to be a new North American nation, and since Britain used Canada as a staging ground in the war the Colonies won, why not?

After first offering eastern Canada (modern-day Québec), Hartley reneged; his opening parlay, including rights to the Newfoundland fisheries (the Grand Banks), caused outrage back home, so he backed off, then refused to hand over the British foothold in the New World. (This, in fact, wasn't the first time the Americans had gone after Québec and lost. In August 1775, American troops were defeated at the snowy Battle of Québec, having foolishly invaded under the false assumption that the French population would join them in their fight against the Crown. What they failed to consider, however, was that the existing hostility between Catholics and Protestants was greater than that between the Quebecois and their British rulers.)

Instead, the two sides ultimately agreed (after more than a year of negotiations) to draw a northern border "from the Atlantic, through the Great Lakes, to the northwestern-most point of the Lake of the Woods, and thence on a due west course to the River Mississippi." That this line was imaginary and ill-defined, passing through mostly unexplored woodlands, was left to be sorted out later, a bit of sloppy hand waving that set the stage for a century's worth of border skirmishes without diminishing the sense that America was somehow "owed" what became, in 1791, the provinces of Upper and Lower Canada, then, in 1840, the united Province of Canada.

Fig.2: Much of the friendliest border in the world—and the longest, at 5,525 miles—is a twenty-foot-wide mowed strip along the 45th parallel (or, later, as the United States expanded westward, the 49th parallel).

SUCCESS IS INEVITABLE

Almost as soon as Upper and Lower Canada were created, anti-Canada War Hawks, led by hothead Henry Clay, representative from Kentucky and Speaker of the House (nickname: "The Dictator"), were spoiling for a fight as an excuse to seize the new provinces, and Britain obligingly offered one in 1807 when its warship the HMS *Leopard* stopped the USS *Chesapeake* to look for men to "press" into service, since any man "used to sea" was considered fair game for forced conscription into the Royal Navy. The *Leopard* fired on the *Chesapeake*, which immediately surrendered after this grueling one-shot barrage; the commander, James Barron, was later court-martialed and suspended from command. This minor day of infamy was the first beat in drumming up a war with Great Britain that Clay and the Hawks needed, which they finally won on June 18, 1812, the official start of the War of 1812. If naval impressment was the cause, then Canada was the instrument to redress America's injuries. Clay famously proclaimed, "Our wrongs have been great; our cause is just; and if we are decided and firm, success is inevitable."

Clay had reason to be optimistic: the balance of power in 1812 was more equal than in 1776, and the new United States might even have had the upper hand: the US population by this time was 7.7 million, compared to five hundred thousand in Canada. The British had only six thousand troops to the north, and these were spread very thin. American troops were more than double, and the American navy was, on paper at least, the equal of the Royal Navy (assuming commanders who, like Barron, didn't surrender after the first sniff of gunpowder). Most important, Britain was bogged down back home in a war against Napoleon, so President Madison could be excused for thinking this would be a quick war, resulting in the easy annexation of Lower and Upper Canada. Moreover, the population of Lower Canada was two-thirds French and one-third recent American immigrants, and most Upper Canadians were American by birth; British Major General Isaac Brock, worried about whose side they would take, warned that most Upper Canadians were "essentially bad," or "so completely American as to rejoice in the prospects of a change of Government."

What nobody foresaw, though, was that American troops soldiered like extras from a Laurel and Hardy film.

Fig.3: HMS *Leopard* firing a single shot at USS *Chesapeake*

HULL ATTACKS CANADA, LOSES DETROIT

las, poor General William Hull. Was he an inept strategist worthy of his court-martial, or simply the victim of the spotty delivery of the United States Postal Service?

Hull, a Revolutionary War hero, was commissioned to organize and lead the Army of the Northwest, stationed at Fort Detroit. During Hull's march from Ohio to Detroit, war was declared officially, and a dispatch promptly mailed. The letter failed to reach Hull in time for him to realize that sending a schooner loaded with supplies, baggage, and some wounded up the Maumee River (and ahead of the protection of his troops) was a poor idea. Worse, the schooner carried documents detailing the Americans' secret invasion plans for Canada's Fort Amherstburg, the garrison and shipyard built in 1796 on Bois Blanc Island, south of Mackinac Island at the mouth of the Detroit River in Lake Huron, to discourage a possible American attack on the Great Lakes. British troops, aware of the state of war, courtesy their superior mail system, easily snatched up the schooner and the plans.

Hull arrived in Detroit without supplies or food, and could find there only soap and whiskey. Presumably clean and a bit drunk, two thousand American troops marched on July 12, 1812, from Detroit to Québec City as part of the no-longer-secret American offensive on Amherstburg. President Thomas Jefferson declared that occupying Québec was simply "a matter of marching," but the Americans found themselves outmatched by superior and "been waiting for you" British forces, who had adroitly enlisted the aid of hostile Native Americans—already stripped of their lands in 1804 by the Harrison Land Act and

Fig.4: Massacre at Fort Dearborn

other anti-Indian policies—under the command of the legend-
ary and ruthless Shawnee leader Tecumseh ("Panther Across
the Sky"). Tecumseh famously asked, "Who are the white people that we should fear them? They cannot run fast, and are
good marks to shoot at."

Naively, Hull expected the Lower Canadians to welcome
the Americans as liberators, and to join the Americans in a
fight against "tyranny and oppression," but instead was quickly
pushed back. Opposing him was Major General Isaac Brock himself, who played on Hull's fear of Tecumseh and his "savages,"
sending the message, "It is far from my intention to join in a
war of extermination, but you must be aware that the numerous body of Indians who have attached themselves to my troops
will be beyond control the moment the contest commences."
Allegedly intoxicated, Hull took the bait and surrendered—a

new record, without a shot fired. He was later court-martialed for cowardice and neglect of duty. Sentenced to death, the conviction was commuted due to his advanced age. In his defense, Hull claimed that the Indians were "numerous beyond example, and more greedy of violence...than the Vikings or Huns." Meanwhile, the British offered Tecumseh the rank of brigadier general in the British army and a colorful officer's sash, both of which he politely refused.

Hull's fear of Indians may not have been completely unfounded. Days before surrendering, he ordered the evacuation of Fort Dearborn in Chicago, surrounded by unfriendly Potawatomi Indians. Although the sixty-five militia and army men in the fort were opposed to leaving, their commanding officer, Captain Nathan Heald, felt bound to follow Hull's orders. To pacify the Potawatomi, he offered them the fort and surrounding land, but refused to add the fort's firearms, ammunition, and liquor to the deal. This so infuriated the Indians that five hundred of them stormed Fort Dearborn and killed almost everybody inside. Captain William Wells, a "white Indian," captured as a boy and raised by the Miami, met a particularly grizzly end: the Potawatomi, longtime enemy of the Miami and allies of Tecumseh, beheaded him, carved out his heart, and ate it raw.

UP THE CREEK WITHOUT A PADDLE (LITERALLY): THE AMERICAN ASSAULT ON QUEENSTON

Detroit lost, American forces focused on the capture of Queenston Heights, located on the Canadian side of the Niagara River, now seen as a strategic lynchpin for any successful invasion of the country. Had General Hull not failed, General Stephen Van Rensselaer's assault on Queenston would have been one aspect of a four-pronged attack on British Canada (three strategically important, one a diversionary tactic). As it was, Van Rensselaer's was one of the few attacks that actually launched—a resounding success, all things considered.

Regrettably, poor intelligence, poor weather, and army desertion all worked together to ensure a devastating and bloody defeat for Van Rensselaer's forces. On October 9, 1812, the Americans received a faulty report that Major General Brock, the now celebrated commander of the region's British forces, had raced back to Detroit. Van Rensselaer prepared his troops for attack while his enemy was helmless. Brock however, had only been called away for the day, and was already back at camp by evening.

Van Rensselaer called in militia from nearby stations (who so far had avoided orders for battle) to join his forces, but steady rains turned carriage roads into seas of liquid mud, delaying reinforcements by days. Meanwhile, as Van Rensselaer's troops waited to cross the Niagara, the general's lead boatman deserted, rowing away in a vessel holding all the oars for the rest of his invasion flotilla, in spite of Van Rensselaer's rousing speech to his troops, which came off more as postman than Henry V ("Neither rain, snow, or frost will prevent the embarkation") and did nothing to boost morale and resolve.

The actual battle, on October 13, saw disorganized American forces gunned down, sunk, and outflanked, despite greater numbers and stronger positions. It was a bloody, demoralizing mess, no less for the British, who lost Major General Brock to US gunfire.

Fig.5: Major General Brock urging his men forward after being fatally wounded at the Battle of Queenston Heights

LET'S TRY MONTREAL,
OR, THE HEROISM OF DISASTER

On the heels of the failed invasions of Amherstburg and Queenston, Secretary of War William Eustis played his last hand on the Canadian front: an assault on Montreal, under the command of Major General Henry Dearborn, another aging Revolutionary War hero. He was known affectionately by his troops as "Granny," in reference to his corpulence and, possibly, his need to get everything arranged just so before the raiding party began. Eustis urged him forward: "Congress must not meet without a victory to announce to them," the increasingly worried war secretary pleaded. On a night in November, Dearborn sent a scouting party of five hundred from his army of six thousand men into Canada, near Lacolle, Québec. Under the cover of darkness, the Americans opened fire on each other, and in the face of such deadly midnight chaos, it's no surprise that the troops still on the American side of the border refused to cross into Canada. With no reinforcements, Dearborn called off the campaign and marched his regiment back to Plattsburgh, New York. His failed assault (on the enemy, anyway) was described by a colleague as a "miscarriage, without even the heroism of disaster."

Defeated on all three fronts, the entire Canadian campaign produced nothing but "disaster, defeat, disgrace, and ruin and death," complained the *Green-Mountain Farmer*, a Vermont newspaper. Treasury Secretary Albert Gallatin wrote to Jefferson, "The series of misfortunes exceeds all anticipations made even by those who had the least confidence in our inexperienced officers and undisciplined men."

Fig.6: USS *Constitution* sinking HMS *Guerrière* off the coast of Nova Scotia, August 19, 1812

Happily for the Americans, the sailing was smoother on the seas, where the American navy more than held its own against the Royal Navy, feared in its day as the "Mistress of the Seas" but now spread very thin around the globe as it fought the French in Europe and tried to keep open lucrative trade routes in the Caribbean. The brightest moment of the naval war came when the USS *Constitution* chased down and sank the HMS *Guerrière*. In this battle, at least one British cannonball bounced off the thick hull of the *Constitution*, earning her the nickname "Old Ironsides."

The *Constitution*'s victory at sea was the morale-turning boost the Americans needed, and a huge blow to British pride. In more than two hundred battles at sea in the prior two decades, Britain had lost only five. The stunned London *Evening Star* described the upstart American navy as "a few fir-built frigates manned by a handful of bastards and outlaws," and popular opinion in Britain quickly turned against the government's handling of the American war. The *Times* of London railed, "We have suffered ourselves to be beaten in detail by a Power that we should not have allowed to send a vessel to sea."

NAPOLEON, AMERICA'S UNEXPECTED
SMALL-FRY ALLY

Flush with its successes at sea, America put aside its plans to invade Canada, but the tide was about to turn in Britain's favor. In 1814, Napoleon abdicated, following his staggering defeat in Russia, and was exiled to Elba. This freed up Britain to focus on its "other war," in North America. And plenty of Britons were angry enough about the embarrassments at sea to call for revenge. "I have it much at heart," proclaimed Vice Admiral Alexander Cochrane, the new commander of the Atlantic fleet, "to give [the Americans] a complete drubbing before peace is made." "Chastise [*sic*] the savages," urged the *Times*, "for such they are, in a much truer sense, than the followers of Tecumseh."

The Brits very quickly built up their troop strength in Canada, more than tripling the number of men to fifty-two thousand by the end of 1814.

One of the earliest targets of the reinvigorated British troops was Maine, which turned out to be easy pickings. First stop was Eastport on Moose Island. The poorly manned Fort Sullivan surrendered without a shot (tying the previous record). The islanders were offered a choice of taking an oath of allegiance to the Crown or leaving; everybody took the oath.

Next was Castine on Penobscot Bay. Another poorly manned redoubt surrendered (40 Americans in the face of 2,500 British), blowing up their supplies and fleeing into the woods. Undeterred, the British continued up the Penobscot River, met little resistance, and took all territory up to Bangor, then Machias, giving them control of one hundred miles of the Maine coast and most of the territory immediately inland. Once again, most

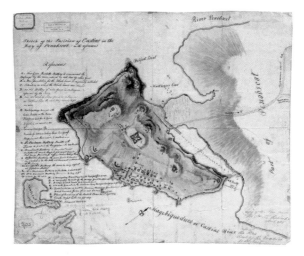

Fig.7: "Sketch of the Position of Castine in the Bay of Penobscot, with references." Capt. Bonneycastle, cartographer, April 1815. NSA, Royal Engineers Office no. R.9. Image shows fortifications in Castine and the newly widened "British Canal."

locals took the oath of allegiance: "It is scarcely conceivable to imagine the joy of the inhabitants," reported the Salem *Essex Register*. Mainers hoped for an end to taxation and easier trade with Canada. Castine quickly became a resort town for British military on leave, and ground zero for trade (that is, smuggling) with the enemy across the Canadian border.

So Washington hit back where it hurt, and, while plotting an invasion to retake the ungrateful territory, suspended mail delivery to occupied Maine. Incredibly enough, this did not bring about the downfall of the British or win back the hearts of Mainers, and eastern Maine remained under British control and allegiance until the end of the war. (When Maine was returned to the States at the end of the war, money collected as customs duties in Castine was taken to Halifax and placed in a special account called the "Castine fund." It was used later to found Dalhousie University.)

With Maine firmly in hand, Britain moved its troops from Canada to the Chesapeake, where they famously occupied Washington, DC, encountering minimal resistance: only five hundred troops who seemed to one British observer "country people, who would have been much more appropriately employed in attending to their agricultural occupations than in standing with their muskets in their hands." These farmer soldiers fled so quickly—in one-hundred-degree muggy DC weather dressed in wool uniforms, to be fair—complained British Major General Robert Ross, that it "precluded the possibility of many prisoners being taken." By eight o'clock on the evening of August 24, 1814, the British walked into an abandoned White House and "speedily consumed" the dinner waiting on the table, presumably laid out for the hastily departed President James Madison and First Lady Dolley. Even though the wine was judged "very good," for a tip, the British set fire to the building before moving on to torch the Capitol building, the Treasury, and the War and State Departments. The blaze could be seen from forty miles away.

Although some Britons were embarrassed by the burning of the city, others rejoiced at the obvious embarrassment of the Americans, who were then further outraged at the follow-up attack on Baltimore, amid reports that British troops pried open coffins looking for booty. "Their conduct would have disgraced cannibals," fumed Congressman Robert Wright.

The effect on the American psyche was deep: "Our affairs," cautioned Navy Secretary William Jones, "are as gloomy as can well be." To make matters worse, morale among Yankee troops plummeted, and desertion became a major problem; almost

13 percent of the army deserted, and executions as a result were higher than in any war since. Worst of all, the young nation was running desperately short of money. There was no cash to pay troops—some were in arrears six to twelve months—and many more mutinied as a result.

The financial crisis reached a peak in 1814, when the US government defaulted on its national debt and stopped specie payments, which ironically had been flowing into Canada to finance British government notes—some $2 million in gold in 1814 alone. The British invasion of the Chesapeake set off a run on banks in the northeast. Without any federal backing, banks

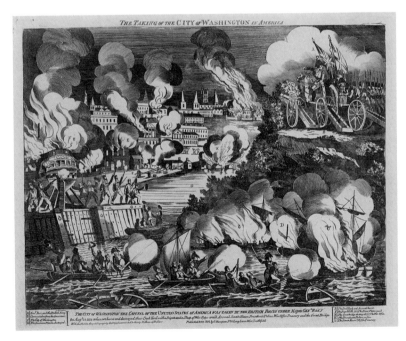

Fig.8: The burning of Washington, DC

refused to honor each other's notes, making it impossible for the government to move money around the country, which, with only increasingly worthless Treasury notes in hand, meant that the administration effectively had no money to fund the war.

What little money remained, especially among British troops keen for British goods, continued flowing into Canada, while Americans bartered to obtain much-needed supplies, and cash, from the north. "Two thirds of the army in Canada," boasted George Prevost, commander in chief of British America, "are at this moment eating beef provided by American contractors, drawn principally from the states of New York and Vermont." Some New England farmers marched their cattle to the Canadian border, where a Canadian smuggler lured them across with a basket of grain. Trade with both Canada and British-occupied Maine flourished (Castine was now a major port of entry), along with military intelligence.

Rampant trade with the enemy, the lack of money and men, and the growing economic emergency weighed heavily on the president, who was described by an associate as "miserably shattered and woebegone," especially as popular discontent over the war spread throughout the Northeast (much of the West and some of the Midwest managed to thrive during the war), enough that Madison called an early session of Congress in September 1814 to deal with the crisis.

Meeting in the patent office—the Capitol building destroyed—only soured the mood of the legislators, who complained bitterly about the cramped quarters and "privations" of every sort. Making matters worse were the terms of a peace offer from London demanding territorial concessions in Maine and Minnesota, the creation of an Indian reservation in the Northwest, and an end to American fishing rights in Canadian waters.

Fig.9: The burned-out shell of the Capitol building

In reality, Madison had been seeking a peace treaty since June 18, 1812, the day war was declared, and discussions continued for much of the war (including failed negotiations with Russia as mediator). With America in such deep crisis, though, the British knew they had the upper hand and agreed to a peace conference in Ghent, Belgium, which lasted until Christmas Eve, 1814. Chief American negotiator John Quincy Adams complained that his British counterparts were "arrogant, overbearing, and offensive." The thing that offended them most was the accusation of an American goal of the "conquest of Canada and its permanent annexation to the United States," which Adams and team denied until confronted with written proclamations on the subject by none other than General William Hull, anti-hero of Detroit. Even worse was Britain's proposal to create an Indian buffer zone on the US western frontier, not only to check American expansion, but also to gain favor with their Indian allies in any future war over Canada, which most observers thought inevitable. "Those sable heroes," editorialized the British *Sun*, "must ever be protected against Yankee encroachment and barbarity."

After months of back and forth, the Treaty of Ghent (also known as the Peace of Christmas Eve) ended the War of 1812, in large part by restoring the 1783 border. Considering the poor hand America had to play and the defeatist attitude back home (the *Boston Gazette* conceded that having declared war and failed, the nation must now "pay the price"), it was possible for the Madison administration to spin the treaty as a case of America losing the war but winning the peace. The *Times* of London agreed, in their way, calling the treaty "deadly and disgraceful" for letting the United States off without "a sound flogging."

In their haste to conclude a deal before Christmas, a number of disputes about the precise location of the US-Canada border were left unsettled.

Some say that the War of 1812 is the closest Canada has had to its own war of independence, and helped shape the myth that the British and French populations joined together to fight off an invader from the south, saving the country from foreign conquest and domination. Although, surely, the ineptitude of American soldiers and their commanders helped.

PART TWO

BORDER DISPUTES

THE PORK AND BEANS WAR

With the possible exception of boxed macaroni and cheese, many consider pork and beans to be the United States' greatest contribution to world cuisine. Many early-nineteenth-century lumberjacks certainly did, and pork'n'beans was usually served as a special dinner on Sundays only.

As keen as many Mainers had been during the War of 1812 to do business with Canada, legally or otherwise, in January 1839, the Maine legislature, fed up after decades of arguments about who owned the right to cut down the dense forests on the border with New Brunswick, sent a posse of volunteer militia from Bangor to confiscate the equipment of any New Brunswick lumberjack they could find cutting "their" trees. The Canadians mounted their own posse, captured the Maine militia, and transported them, in chains, to a barracks in Woodstock, New Brunswick.

Pent-up frustration and memories of the not-so-long-ago "Second Revolution" quickly caused the situation to spiral out of control into what's known as the Pork and Beans War, in honor of the lumberjacks' beloved favorite meal. Maine organized another one thousand volunteers, the British sent troops up from the Caribbean, and the Mohawks offered to help the Canadians. By the time the US Congress authorized a force of fifty thousand men and $10 million under the command of General Winfield ("Old Fuss and Feathers") Scott, US Secretary of State Daniel Webster and Chancellor of the Exchequer Baron Ashburton agreed to redraw the border in a way that gave more land to the States than Canada; Ashburton later justified the imbalance

Fig.10: Lumberjacks enjoying pork and beans

by pointing out, "The whole territory we were wrangling about was worth nothing."

Although no shots were fired (and, uncharacteristically, no Americans surrendered as a result), Private Hiram T. Smith is counted as the sole casualty of the Aroostook War, either from freezing to death, drowning, being run over by a supply wagon, trampled by a horse he was sent to feed, or all of the above. A marker to commemorate this fallen hero is on Route 2A in Haynesville, Maine.

The short-lived Pork and Beans War also has the distinction of being the only war in history between an American state and a foreign nation.

THE PIG HEARD 'ROUND THE WORLD

What is it about pork and the Canadian border?

Less than twenty years after the Pork and Beans War, another territorial dispute, also swine-related, erupted on the other side of the continent. Much like when World War I ignited with the shooting of Archduke Franz Ferdinand in Sarajevo, the Pig War began with the shooting of, well, a pig.

The Oregon Treaty of 1846 established the 49th parallel as the boundary between Canada and the rapidly expanding western United States, but left unclear the sovereignty of the San Juan Islands in the Strait of Juan de Fuca, off the coast of Seattle. Both countries quickly claimed the islands, setting the stage for international conflict, Puget Sound–style.

In June 1859, an American farmer-squatter, Lyman Cutlar, saw a large black pig rooting around in his garden, eating potatoes. He promptly chased, shot, and killed the pig, which turned out to be owned by Charles Griffin, manager of a ranch owned by the imperialist British supermerchant-squatter the Hudson's Bay Company (also the owners of most of Western Canada). The ensuing fight over liability and compensation quickly escalated into a military standoff. Following the orders of the local US Army commander, Anglophobe Brigadier General William Selby Harney, Oregon landed sixty-six soldiers under Captain George Pickett (later leader of the ill-fated Pickett's Charge at the Battle of Gettysburg that all but lost the Civil War for the South) just north of the Hudson's Bay ranch in late July, transported there by the US warship USS *Massachusetts*, with its eight thirty-two-pound cannons. The British immediately anchored three warships in Griffin Bay to keep the Americans from occupying

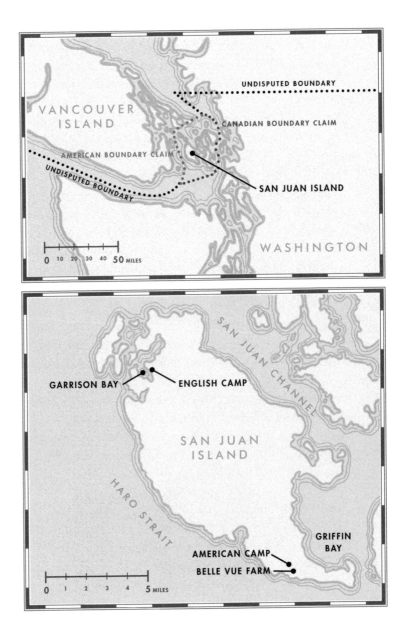

UNDISPUTED BOUNDARY

VANCOUVER
ISLAND

CANADIAN BOUNDARY CLAIM

AMERICAN BOUNDARY CLAIM

UNDISPUTED BOUNDARY

SAN JUAN ISLAND

WASHINGTON

0 10 20 30 40 50 MILES

SAN JUAN CHANNEL

GARRISON BAY

ENGLISH CAMP

SAN JUAN
ISLAND

HARO STRAIT

GRIFFIN
BAY

AMERICAN CAMP

BELLE VUE FARM

0 1 2 3 4 5 MILES

the islands. Both sides upped their positions in rapid succession, and by the end of the summer, Pickett had almost five hundred soldiers with fourteen artillery cannons, while the British increased their force to five warships with more than two thousand men and seventy cannons, echoes of the lopsided Falkland Islands buildup centuries later. With the clear military advantage, the governor of Vancouver Island ordered the British to land and engage the Americans, but Rear Admiral Robert Baynes refused, saying that "to engage two great nations in a war over a squabble about a pig" was foolish. As a result, both sides agreed to reduce their forces to one hundred men each, housed in two camps, the British on the north end of San Juan Island and the Americans on the south. These camps were maintained, and the conflict simmered until resolved by arbitration in the early 1870s. The British withdrew their troops in 1872, the Americans in 1874. The remnants of both camps are preserved today at the San Juan Island National Historical Park. In spite of all the saber rattling, no shots were fired and the "war" ended peacefully, which leads at least one historian to call the Pig War "the most perfect war in history." To be accurate, though, one shot was fired, and one life lost: that of the anonymous pig.

Fig.11: American camp on San Juan Island

TRADE YOU ALABAMA FOR CANADA

Although Britain was officially neutral in the American Civil War, this meant only that they continued to do business with both sides, selling supplies to the North and buying desperately needed cotton for England's productive mills from the South. Most famously, though, Britain built and sold the Confederacy the warship CSS *Alabama*, described as one of the most well-crafted warships ever built. Two-hundred-thirty-feet long, the 1,050-ton sloop could sail under wind (with three tall masts) or steam power (with two three-hundred-horsepower engines and a retractable screw propeller). A crew of 24 officers and 120 men could rove and raid, which they did with ruthless effectiveness, boarding 450 Union ships, destroying or burning 66 of them, most of which were merchant marine. She took a total of two thousand prisoners without a single loss to her company. The *Alabama* was a source of furious public resentment north of the Mason-Dixon line, particularly in early 1863, when it sank the USS *Griswold*, a relief ship filled with flour and corn headed for Britain, aid for Lancashire's suffering cotton workers. The Union responded to the sinking of the *Griswold*, flying the flags of both nations, by drawing up plans to declare war on Britain. Ultimately, these were scrapped, as the North already had its hands plenty full, but anti-British sentiment hit a fever pitch. Massachusetts Senator Charles Sumner warned, "The feeling towards England runs high, and I hear it constantly said that war is inevitable unless these ships now building are kept from preying on our commerce." The *New York Times* chimed in, saying, "England will be hated for it, till the last American now on the stages goes to his grave."

Fig.12: Captain Raphael Semmes aboard the CSS *Alabama*

It's little surprise, then, that the victorious Union sought reparations from Britain for the damage wreaked by the *Alabama*, to the tune of hundreds of millions of dollars, along with a formal apology. Britain was not about to apologize to its former upstart colony, nor could it afford to pay reparations, even had it been willing, as its economy was gravely wounded by the shortage of Southern cotton during the Civil War.

President Ulysses S. Grant, who firmly believed that Canada would become part of the United States during his term, proposed trading Canada for the *Alabama* claims. Secretary of State Hamilton Fish delivered this offer to British Ambassador Sir Edward Thornton, requesting "the removal of the British flag" from North America to "render easy the settlement of all other questions between the two governments."

Britain demurred, and in a great stroke of irony, the *Alabama* claims were settled in 1870 as part of a three-way negotiation with the United States, Britain, and Canada over American fishing rights, in which Britain expressed "regret," but no apology. The British granted the States access to Canadian waters, for which the States paid $5.5 million, effectively paying Britain's North American colony to resolve its own outstanding Civil War–related issues.

Soon after the Civil War, Secretary of State William Henry Seward, in a bid to try and force Britain to make territorial concessions to the States, played on popular opinion that Britain had sided with the Confederacy. Seward heard rumors of support in British Columbia for annexation by America (rumors, in fact, started by American traders there, but not necessarily shared by Canadians or Métis—the offspring of French and English traders and women from the First Nations, Canada's aboriginal peoples), which made him wonder whether the States could just buy western Canada. "The line of difference between the two countries was becoming thinner and thinner....Assuming any tolerable share of good will, there was no reason why earnest efforts might not eliminate it altogether," he wrote.

Fig.13: America's check for the purchase of Alaska

Seward was already negotiating with the Russians to buy "Russian North America," that is, Alaska, which they wanted to unload fearing it would be seized anyway in the event of a war with Britain. The Russians, hard up for cash, offered first to sell it to Britain, but when they declined, offered it to the Americans as early as 1859; in 1867 Seward negotiated the purchase for $7.2 million, about two cents per acre, though not enough of a bargain to keep Alaska from being known as "Seward's Folly." For Russia, this had the added benefit of surrounding British Columbia with American territory, weakening the British position in the event of another war between them (following the Crimea). In similar pincer-like thinking, Seward also approached Denmark in 1867 about buying Greenland, which would have completely surrounded Canada with American territory. (Weirdly, this idea resurfaced in 1946, when the United States again offered to buy Greenland from Denmark, to keep Germany from building bases there.)

The purchase of Alaska was seen as an easy first step to acquiring British Columbia and then, eventually, all of Canada. The idea of annexation reached its fever pitch with House Resolution 754, the Bill to Annex Canada into the United States, introduced into Congress by Massachusetts Representative Nathaniel Banks in 1866. It involved paying the Hudson's Bay Company $10 million for its lands, assuming up to $85 million in Canadian public debt, and investing another $50 million to upgrade the Canadian canal system (presumably to integrate it better with American trading routes). The bill was never voted on, dying a quiet death in committee.

TRADE YOU CANADA FOR IRELAND

I n a page straight from a Gilbert and Sullivan libretto of international relations, a group of Irish Catholic loyalists, mostly Civil War vets, founded in 1858 the US fraternal wing of the Irish Republican Brotherhood, operating under the name Fenian Brotherhood, but also calling themselves the Irish Republican Army (the first known instance of that name), based on their "intense and undying hatred toward the monarchy and oligarchy of Great Britain." They had little trouble attracting money and followers; by the end of 1865, the Fenians had nearly $500,000 and about ten thousand American Civil War veterans organized in secret military clubs throughout the States.

Their "intense hatred" led them to hatch a scheme to occupy and seize Canada as a hostage to force the British to withdraw from Ireland in exchange. Or, at least, to proclaim an Irish Republic on Canadian soil, or to establish a base to launch an overseas invasion of Ireland, or, even better, to encourage the United States to follow with additional troops and annex Canada. Although Secretary of State Seward gave tacit support to the idea of an Irish Republic on North American soil (in a bald appeal to Irish American voters, totaling 1.6 million people), the Fenians completely misread the equation on the northern side of the border. Expecting (once again) to be welcomed by the Canadians, they overlooked the fact that most Canadian Irish were, in fact, Protestants from Northern Ireland, not Catholics (outside Québec, where the Hibernians, another Irish brotherhood, sympathized with the Americans and even lobbied for annexation to the United States to break Canada's ties to Britain), and, having experienced the Famine

Fig.14: Fenian monument in Queen's Park, Toronto

Fig.15: Advertisement for Fenian collars

in Ireland during the 1840s, unlikely to risk their new situation to support the invaders.

In April 1866, the Fenians invaded Indian Island in New Brunswick to set up a staging ground for a subsequent invasion of Campobello Island as well as a possible landing in Ireland itself. By declaring themselves a republic at war with Great Britain, the Fenians hoped to attain the status of belligerents, rather than pirates, and avoid violating US neutrality laws. The Canadian militia, backed up by British gunboats, chased the Fenians off with little effort and no reported casualties.

Lesson not learned, on June 1, 1866, the Fenians tried again, and floated one thousand men in canal boats from Buffalo to Fort Erie, Ontario, part of a planned five-pronged invasion of Canada from New York, Illinois, Wisconsin, Vermont, and the St. Lawrence River. Perhaps overconfident after their easy victory at Indian Island, the Canadians were easily defeated at Ridgeway. The approach of a large detachment of Canadian troops, though, sent the Fenians scurrying back across the border, where they were arrested for, in the words of President Andrew Johnson, "proceedings which constitute a high misdemeanor, forbidden by the laws of the United States as well as by the law of nations." In spite of Johnson's rhetoric, the Fenians were quickly released.

Emboldened by their short-lived success at Ridgeway, the "IRA" launched a series of raids on Canadian targets over the next five years, including planting an Irish flag in the Canadian village of Pigeon Hill (with another force of one thousand men), a symbolic move, but an ineffective footnote in the history of Irish "liberation."

The Fenians tried a better-organized version of this same raid on Montreal on May 24 (Queen's Day) in 1870 from Franklin,

Vermont, where they had amassed an astonishing arsenal of fifteen thousand weapons and three million rounds of small-arms ammunition. Not coincidentally, on the same day, President Grant issued a proclamation upholding the US Neutrality Act of 1818, which meant the government would stop looking the other way at the Fenians' Canadian incursions. In 1871, the Fenians tried again, this time in Manitoba with only forty men, and were quickly suppressed by American authorities. This was the last Fenian raid, and Ireland remained part of the United Kingdom until 1922.

Fig.16: Fenians square off against British troops
at the Battle of Ridgeway

DOMINION DAY

Due in some part to the unifying effect the Fenian raids had on their Canadian subjects—for whom the raids were every bit as upsetting as the CSS *Alabama* had been to the Union—the British passed the British North America Act on July 1, 1867, Dominion Day. Later renamed the Constitution Act, it created a new dominion out of the provinces of New Brunswick (home to the United Empire Loyalists), a somewhat reluctant Nova Scotia (unhappy about paying the same tax rates as their new brethren), and the Province of Canada (the result of the 1840 merger of Upper and Lower Canada, now split into Ontario and Québec). It also promised to sell the new nation Rupert's Land, the enormous landholdings—1.5 million miles square—of the Hudson's Bay Company that covered most of western modern-day Canada (including Manitoba, Saskatchewan, southern Alberta, and Nunavut); northern Ontario and Québec; as well as parts of Minnesota, Montana, and North and South Dakota—another bit of border fuzziness to be sorted out at another time.

It's unclear whether this came as a surprise to the United States, but prevailing wisdom was that it didn't matter, that the new country to the north would not survive long and would, inevitably, be absorbed into its larger, richer, and more powerful neighbor to the south. The *Times* of London, perhaps with sour grapes in mouth, warned that Canada would not survive without "the body, the vital organs, the circulation and the muscular force that are to give adequate power to these widespread limbs." The *New York Times* agreed: "When the experiment of the 'Dominion' shall have failed, as fail it must, a process of peaceful absorption will give Canada her proper place in the Great North American republic."

The *St. Paul Press* astutely recognized in this a blueprint for the de facto future annexation of Canada: "If politically [the Northwest] belongs to Canada, geographically and commercially, it belongs to Minnesota. Canadian policy may propose, but American enterprise will dispose."

Eugene Wheeler, owner of the *St. Paul Press*, wasn't the only border-stater beating the drum about Canada. In Michigan, state senator Zachariah Chandler warned, "This continent is our land and we may as well notify the world...that we will fight for it." The growing American railways were prepared to play hardball, too: the president of the Northern Pacific Railway warned a leading Canadian railway developer that the route of the Northern Pacific was planned close to the border to prevent Canada from taking control of the Western Territories, where there was already interest (some fueled by American bribes) in joining the States. Indeed, Winnipeg's largest hotel, Emmerling's, flew the Stars and Stripes rather than the Union Jack.

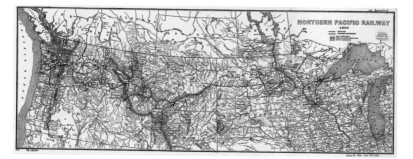

Fig.17: Map of the Union Pacific Railway circa 1900

Hamilton Fish, secretary of state to President Grant, smelling the prevailing wind and hoping to avoid war, tried the direct approach: he asked Edward Thornton, British ambassador in Washington, how the annexation of Canada might be seen in London? The British, he was told, had no particular desire to hold onto Canada, and if Canada wanted to go, the Empire would stand aside.

This kind of bellicose saber rattling and backroom politicking surely worried some Canadians, and infuriated the new prime minister, Sir John A. Macdonald, who was busily building a coast-to-coast nation to rival the United States, at least in size if not in economic and military might. Canada was still abjectly poor, largely agricultural, and without a standing army, other than the recently formed North West Mounted Police (rechristened the Royal Canadian Mounted Police in 1904), numbering only 309 men, 300 horses, 50 cows, and 40 calves (better equipped to corral rogue American whisky runners or a few unhappy traders at the Red River Colony); a "Permanent Active Militia"; and a handful of voluntary militia units. Even combined, the RCMP and the full strength of Canada's militia forces would not be enough to stave off an invasion from a now-idle Union Army of five hundred thousand seasoned veterans.

Canada—without its own official army until dragged, by treaty, into Britain's Boer War in 1899—was wholly dependent on the protection of the British, who were, at best, ambivalent about how much support their former colony could expect: although the official line was that Britain would "defend every part of the Empire with all the resources at its command," General Michel, commanding officer of all military forces in Canada, concluded in 1867 (before retiring back to London) that post–Civil War reconstruction in the United States (along with the larger project of suppressing Indians in its own West) made it unlikely that America would turn its army north, and worried that the continued presence of British troops might instead be seen mistakenly as a provocation to Washington. Accordingly, he recommended that British troops be cut from fifteen thousand to just six thousand. In 1869, this shrank to only two thousand, and, by 1871, British military presence in Canada ended entirely, but for a few sailors guarding the Royal Navy base in Halifax. Canada was left with only Britain's verbal assurance that it would come to the rescue if the United States decided to try and annex its northern neighbor, as so many on both sides of the border assumed it would. Meanwhile, back home, most Britons seemed to feel that Canada was on its own, and many thought, quite openly, that the colony, dirt poor, would be much better off as part of its wealthy, powerful, and rapidly modernizing neighbor. The American "annexation" of Texas from Mexico—in 1845—certainly gave Canadians something to ponder, and lay the foundation for a deep suspicion of America's intentions toward its northern neighbor.

Despite any possible feelings of abandonment and fears of an encroaching and ravenous United States, Canadians still found reason to hold their chins high. The Trent Affair of 1861 sparked the threat of another war between the United States and Britain, when a Union ship intercepted a British mail packet carrying two Southern diplomats heading for Great Britain to urge diplomatic recognition of the Confederacy. Immediate reaction in the Union was a call for war on England, an action Abraham Lincoln could ill afford. The governor general of Canada, Charles Stanley, acted on his own and moved men and weapons to the border. He did this quietly, not to keep it secret from the Americans, but to avoid panic among Canadians.

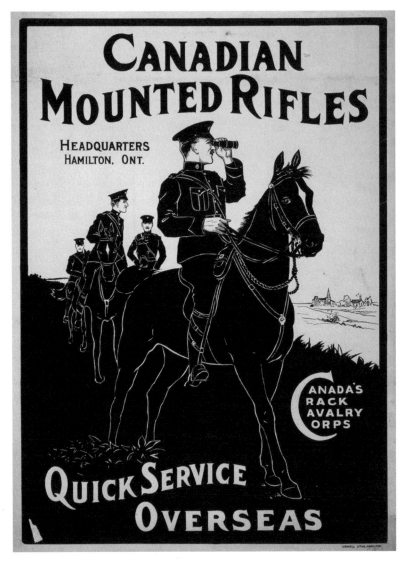

Fig.18: Recruitment poster for the Canadian Mounted Rifles, 1914

Of course, news of his troop movements reached Washington, where Seward was warned by his agent in London that Britain was convinced Seward had masterminded the Trent affair to provoke a war that would allow the United States to invade Canada, and that British dockyards were "alive with war supplies" being gathered and sent to Canada as reinforcements (at this point, Britain was ready to make good on its claim to defend the Empire).

Rumors of an imminent invasion swept through Canada, and Macdonald used them to organize some 450 militia units, 46,000 men, and to unite Canadians, especially Maritimers, in common cause. Benefit concerts, fundraisers, and student rifle corps brought Canadians together in the face of a war that seemed only days away. The Trent affair festered and the buildup continued until President Lincoln decided, on Christmas Day, 1861, that he "preferred to fight one war at a time," acknowledging that a war with Britain would be disastrous and work to the advantage of the Confederacy. Fingers continued to be pointed even after Lincoln's death. In fact, the United States accused Canada of involvement in the Lincoln assassination, linking John Wilkes Booth back to Montreal and what was know as the "Confederate's Canadian Cabinet," where Lincoln was much loathed. Canada countered, taking the allegations as Washington again looking for an excuse to declare war.

Canadian nationalism reached its fever pitch with the onset of World War I in 1914. Although obligated by treaty to send troops to support Britain in its war effort, a surge of Empire pride resulted in a flood of thirty-three thousand volunteers, seven thousand more than required, though almost universally without training or experience.

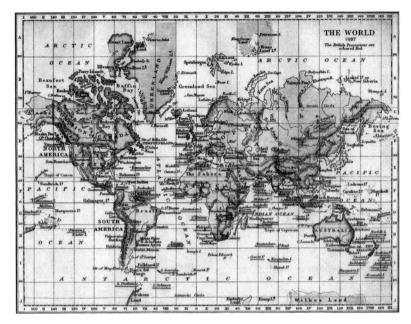

Fig.19: Half the world colored pink: the British Empire
before World War I

Historians Cathryn Corns and John Hughes-Wilson explain in their history of the Great War, *Blindfold and Alone*, that Canada's exuberant nationalism "sprang not just from Darwinian ideas of racial superiority and Nietzchean influences on educated thought, but also from the unifying symbol of the 'British Empire.' British national consciousness was inextricably entwined with imperial glory, rights, and responsibilities.... The Empire was a source of stability, self-belief in their superiority, pride, or stern duty. Half the globe coloured pink really meant something in a way we today find incomprehensible, if not downright embarrassing.... It is almost impossible for us to realize just how strong a unifying feature the 'Empire' was.

Imperial ties were a genuine force in 1914 and were sufficient enough to pull hundreds of thousands of new Canadians, Australians, New Zealanders, and South Africans from the white colonial dominions back across the oceans to volunteer to fight—and die—for the 'mother' country."

The Canadian victory at Vimy Ridge, on Easter Day, 1917, where French troops had failed and died by the thousands during the two preceding years, cemented the Canadian sense of nationhood, and certainly impressed a young Lieutenant Colonel James Sutherland Brown, who, like many others, saw the Canadian triumph as a "great battle," won through exceptional planning, training, and courageous fighting, and, quite possibly, evidence that Canadian troops, even without the experience, training, and materiel of their European counterparts, could prevail against a larger and better-equipped army.

Fig.20: Canadian victors at Vimy Ridge

PART THREE

WE'VE GOT YOUR BACK:

WAR PLAN RED & DEFENCE SCHEME NO. 1

CANADA FIRST

As Canada's first prime minister, Sir John A. Macdonald, successfully pieced together a sea-to-shining-sea country to match America in size—complete with construction of a scandal-plagued railroad, the Canadian Pacific—a sense of national pride emerged in the start-up country. Not surprisingly, at least some of this was in comparison to the United States. A group calling themselves "Canada Firsters" saw little contest between their manly new country and the foppish one to the south. "We are a Northern people...more manly, more real, than the weak-marrowed bones and superstitions of an effeminate South." This also carried racist overtones: Canada was stocked with sturdy Northern Europeans (Saxons, Celts, Danes, Germans, and Scandinavians), while the States were watered down with "vagrant populations of Italy and other countries of Southern Europe." Indeed, one noted historian, writer, and United Empire Loyalist suggested that what Canada really needed to prove its new macho identity was a "rattling good war with the United States."

Fig. 21: Donald Alexander Smith, cofounder of the Canadian Pacific Railway, driving the last spike to signify the end of construction and the union of the Dominion of Canada

BUSTER BROWN

t's hard to imagine a family that better encapsulates the history, contradictions, and politics of the early Canadian dominion than that of James Sutherland "Buster" Brown.

Brown's great-grandfather emigrated from Scotland to Massachusetts, then moved to Canada as part of the United Empire Loyalist (UEL) migration during the American Revolution. His son, Augustus, moved to Simcoe, Ontario, where his son, Frank, was born in 1848. Frank ran the second-largest egg exporting business in Canada, selling 248,000 dozen to the United States in 1889 alone—primarily to Buffalo and New York City—making him more of a "continentalist," unconcerned with his American customers when business was good, and less worried about politics than his pro-British father and, as things turned out, son, James, known as "Buster."

Simcoe was, and still is, a prosperous town ninety miles (147 km) southwest of Toronto, not far from Lake Erie. Largely destroyed in the War of 1812 (and subsequently rebuilt), Simcoe is not far from Ridgeway, Ontario, site of one of the final Fenian raids. This might explain why, at school, young Buster and his friends played at "repelling American invaders rather than cowboys and Indians," according to a reminiscence by his son.

How much his grandfather's Tory politics, or recent memories of Fenian raids, influenced Brown's future attitudes about the United States is only a matter for psycho-historical speculation. We do know, however, that by the age of fourteen, Buster was ready to repel invaders for real and joined the 39th Norfolk Rifles, Simcoe's proud volunteer militia, as a boy bugler, something that surely would have required his father's approval.

Fig.22: Portrait of a young Buster Brown

Fig.23: Headquarters of the 39th Norfolk Rifles,
Simcoe, Ontario

The 39th Norfolk Rifles was the beginning of Brown's auspicious military career, which he pursued while teaching in nearby Port Rowan and, for a brief period, studying law. Brown's real passion, though, was the army. He rose quickly through the ranks, first in the militia (achieving the rank of sergeant at the age of eighteen), and subsequently in the Royal Canadian Regiment (RCR) (at only twenty-five), one of Canada's oldest "Permanent Force" military units. In the RCR, Brown was recognized for his outstanding staff and organizational skills. According to his son, Atholl, it was at this time that Brown developed a "definite bias" against the United States, believing that it had a "baleful influence on Canada, and even presented a military threat." His success in the RCR won him admission to the prestigious military college at Camberly, in Surrey, England, a training camp for future officers. Brown's stay at Camberly, however, was cut short by the outbreak of World War I, and he was called back to Canada in August 1914.

As soon as he reached home, Brown was appointed acting director of military operations at Militia HQ, where he organized the deployment of the newly formed Canadian Expeditionary Force (CEF), some 31,000 men and 7,600 horses, along with associated guns, artillery, wagons, munitions, and vehicles. This he accomplished by commandeering twenty-eight ocean liners, ships better suited for passengers than heavy equipment. Although a junior officer with no large-scale experience in logistics (unless his father's ability to move a quarter-million dozen eggs across international borders somehow rubbed off), Brown performed exceptionally well, enough to be made quickly deputy assistant and quartermaster general of the First Canadian Division and promoted to major, remarkable for a thirty-three-year-old militiaman.

What Brown saw while organizing the Canadian deployment to the European trenches of the Great War was a shocking lack of preparedness: for example, there were no floors for the tents, pitched in heavy rain on fields of deep, chalky mud; no standings for horses; a shortage of clothing; and inferior, if not shoddy, equipment, much of it specified as a result of political patronage back in Ottawa. For example, the MacAdam trenching shovel was patented by Ena MacAdam, personal secretary to the Canadian Minister of Militia Sam Hughes. Even worse was the Ross rifle, which Brown had already reported against in his first days in the RCR; Britain quickly began replacing the Ross with the superior Enfield, itself in short supply as the war dragged on.

In spite of Canadian successes on the battlefield, most famously at Vimy Ridge, and the evolving reputation of the CEF as an "elite" force, Brown saw firsthand the carnage that resulted from inadequate planning and vowed not to let this happen on his watch in his future career as a Canadian military professional. On his return to Canada in 1920, he was named director of military operations and intelligence. From this post, he was able to marry his battlefield experience with his suspicion of the United States to develop a contingency plan in case war broke out between America and Great Britain, a plan of attack disingenuously named Defence Scheme No. 1.

DEFENCE SCHEME NO. 1

With the end of a hugely unpopular war (the War of 1812 being far worse than Vietnam) and the economic chaos that went with it, America quickly entered an age of prosperity. Since journalists and historians like Big Labels to name periods of obvious change, the *Boston Gazette* called these happy days "The Era of Good Feelings." Happier at home meant friendlier overseas, and warming relations with the British were labeled The Great Rapprochement, which became the foundation of the "Special Relationship" that allegedly still defines US-British relations today, set in stone in 1859 when the US Navy came to the aid of the British in the Second Opium War with China.

Although there was still a sense among some Britons that America was an ill-behaved, if not insolent, child with the nerve to "strike his father," the Special Relationship survived a critical test when the United States joined the Allied cause in World War I in 1917.

Although the United States joined the war late in the game, it offered Britain considerable financial help from the start. When the smoke cleared, the Crown owed its former colony, enemy, and, most recently, ally, $22 billion. This is a large sum even by today's standards, but was a staggering amount at the time: consider that Great Britain's entire gross domestic product was only $27 billion. Britain's ability to repay its war debt, therefore, was entirely dependent on Germany's payment of war reparations, which was intermittent at best. Germany defaulted in 1923, causing France to send troops into the Ruhr until a settlement plan was proposed by the United

Fig.24: The Era of Good Feelings, the beginning of the Special Relationship between the United States and Britain

States and accepted by all parties. In fact, these loans remain unpaid to this day.

Britain was irritated, reported the US military attaché in London in an August 1920 communiqué, by America's insistence on full repayment of the war debt (in gold or cash, no less!) and by Washington's attitude of "splendid isolation and aloofness." He warned that, for Britain, "America is getting to be too serious a rival. England is convinced that she cannot crush America, therefore she will try to block us at every possible turn, and will endeavor to surround us with potential enemies....There is hardly a shadow of doubt that England is keeping up the closest and friendliest contact with Mexico, Japan and South America and is gradually lining them up against us."

Fig.25: James Sutherland Brown and his "espionage" cohorts scout upstate New York for possible invasion

Little did the attaché know, war planning against the United States was already under way, in the form of the slightly disingenuously named Defence Scheme No. 1, a plan against an imagined war with the United States, Europe, Japan, or a combination of one or more of these, which foresaw an American invasion of Canada as a first step in the next global conflict. Not directly sanctioned by the British military, who saw the defense of Canada as difficult, if not impossible, Defence Scheme No. 1, finalized in 1921, was the brainchild of the Lieutenant Colonel James "Buster" Brown.

Popularly portrayed as a bit of a loose cannon, but actually acting on orders from the chief of general staff, who shared his suspicions about America, Brown (no relation to the comic or children's shoes of the same name) seems to have been inspired by Buster Keaton, as he and four fellow officers under his command donned disguises, loaded into their Model T, and began an espionage mission along the Canada–New England border. Brown, in his full, waxed Victorian mustache, pointed his Kodak at every lock, bridge, and highway they spotted and filled his notebooks with insights that read more like notes for a comic novel than military intelligence. These include:

- The people of Burlington, Vermont, seem "very affable and not as 'American' as other US cities one has visited."
- In rural Vermont he noted that "if [Americans] are not actually lazy, they have a very deliberate way of working and apparently believe in frequent rests and gossip."
- "The women throughout the rural districts appear to be a heavy and not very comely lot."
- Similarly, a large number of men of the state (Vermont) are "fat and lazy but pleasant and congenial."
- In a comical echo of William Hull, Buster was convinced that invading Canadians would be welcomed, if not as liberators, then at least as bartenders, since Vermonters were eager for the drink Prohibition denied them. Asking a local to identify Camel's Hump, one of Vermont's highest peaks, Brown quipped, "You people here are like the camel, you can go seven days without a drink."
- He did find a "large and influential number of American citizens who are not altogether pleased with democracy and have a sneaking regard for Great Britain, British Law, and Constitution, and general civilization." On the whole, Vermont was at best "an obstruction" for any invading Canadian force.

In developing his plan, Brown leaned heavily on his experience in the Great War, especially the German tactic of *Stosstruppen*, precursor to the Blitzkrieg of World War II: quick attacks on an enemy's weak points with small groups of

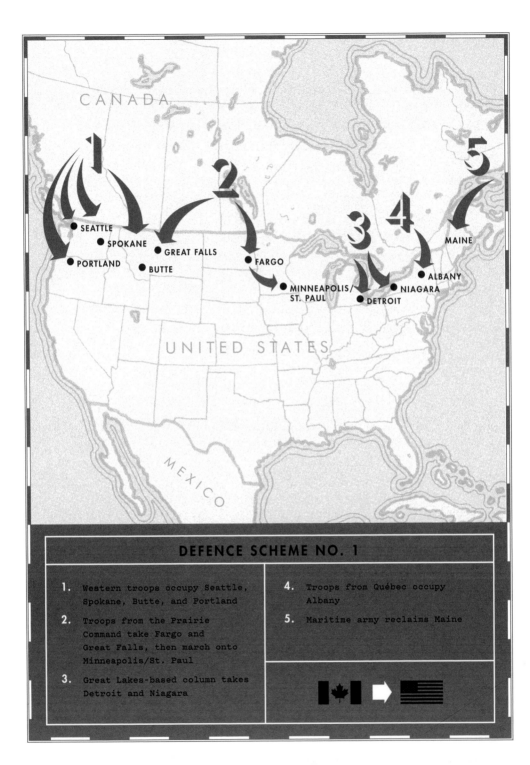

DEFENCE SCHEME NO. 1

1. Western troops occupy Seattle, Spokane, Butte, and Portland

2. Troops from the Prairie Command take Fargo and Great Falls, then march onto Minneapolis/St. Paul

3. Great Lakes-based column takes Detroit and Niagara

4. Troops from Québec occupy Albany

5. Maritime army reclaims Maine

infantry. Brown's goal was to dance like a butterfly and sting like a bee, invade quickly with "flying columns" of militia across the border, then retreat, blowing up bridges and train tracks behind him in an effort to buy time for Canada while Britain sailed to the rescue.

Brown's was a five-pronged attack: With air support, western troops would occupy Seattle, Spokane, Butte, and Portland. Troops from the Prairie Command would take Fargo and Great Falls before moving on to Minneapolis/St. Paul. In the east, troops marching from Québec would occupy Albany, while the Maritime army reclaimed Maine for the Crown. In the Midwest, the Great Lakes Command would take Niagara and Detroit.

Even Brown recognized that "in the defence of Canada… we lack depth," but argued that "depth can only be gained by Offensive Action. To carry out an Offensive Action against the United States, with our population in a ratio of one to twelve and the United States' Regular Army of 175,000 Enlisted Men, and with between two and four millions of men who were lately embodied for service, is a difficult and on the surface an almost hopeless task, but on further study, it would be found out that it is not as hopeless as it appears on the surface." Brown traveled the country pitching his plan to top military brass in, enough that fellow World War I vet and lieutenant governor of British Columbia, George Pearkes, called the scheme a "fantastic desperate plan [that] just might have worked. The Americans had very few troops close to the border. We might have been able to divert their forces to the flanks, and to hold them out of central Canada, until Britain intervened, or second thoughts prevailed in Washington." Others thought it harebrained at best, and Brown's immediate successor, Andrew McNaughton, ordered all copies of the scheme, including Brown's recon notes, burned.

Only fragments of the document remain today, at the Queenston Library in Ontario.

Brown's scheme is not as crazy as it might now seem, even with the lopsided troop figures. The United States had only just demobilized following World War I, a profoundly unpopular war with long tentacles (1.5 million Americans saw combat, and fifty-three thousand died), and what little materiel woefully unprepared America brought to the European theater—indeed, many American soldiers arrived in France without weapons— was still overseas or destroyed. While it seems unlikely that a war-weary United States would have surrendered to Canada without a fight, it's quite possible that the element of surprise might've drawn out Brown's holding action plan. In fact, eighteen years after Brown's *Mouse That Roared* scheme, Finland held off an invasion by its own superpower neighbor, Russia, even though Russia had three times as many soldiers, thirty times as many aircraft, and a hundred times as many tanks. If Canada had its own General Risto Ryti, the Finnish prime minister who outfoxed Stalin—someone like MacDonald—Canada could very well have harassed or held off an American counterattack.

(right) Fig.26: Cover sheet, Defence Scheme No. 1,
signed by James Sutherland Brown

JSB/TB

VERY SECRET.   H.Q. S.3495.

                                            COPY No. 1

DEPARTMENT OF MILITIA AND DEFENCE.

OPERATION CIRCULAR LETTER No.5.   Ottawa, April 29th, 1921.

To -

Defence Scheme No.1.

                    With reference to the special note
at the top of page 1 of Defence Scheme No.1,
the Chief of the General Staff, after due
consideration, has decided that you may show
the Defence Scheme in its entirety to the
General Staff Officer of your District.

                    I am directed to inform you before
showing this scheme to your General Staff Officer the necessity of absolute secrecy must
be impressed upon him, as there are matters
in the Defence Scheme which if conveyed to
certain people, they might make political cap-
ital out of it, besides also the possibility
of the knowledge of this scheme falling into
the hands of possible enemies of this country.

                                    Colonel,
                        Director of Military Operations
                              and Intelligence,
                        for Chief of the General Staff.

DISTRIBUTION LIST -

Copy No.1 to M.D.1
     2   2
     3   3
     4   4
     5   5
     6   6
     7   7
     8   C.G.S.
     9   D.M.O.& I.
    10   10
    11   11
    12   12
    13   13
    14   Binder.
    15   A.G.
    16   Q.M.G.
    17   H.Q.file.

Unaware of Brown's scheme, the report from London convinced American military planners to draw up their own plan in the event of renewed conflict with the largest empire on Earth. For the American War Office, it was clear that any attack from the British would involve their dominion and ally to the north, Canada. In May 1930, the War Plans Division drew up War Plan Red, ostensibly an exercise in "peacetime preparedness," but one that took seriously the idea that Britain's jealousy over America's increasing presence on the world stage, particularly in trade, would, sooner or later, result in an attack on America's merchant marine and foreign trade. This would be followed by a Canada-based invasion of the Great Lakes and manufacturing cities of the Northeast; the governmental and financial centers of Washington, DC, New York, and Pittsburgh; as well as a takeover of the Panama Canal and American interests in the West Indies and the Philippines.

Britain, the War Office declared, had the means to do it, with the world's most powerful navy. Within forty days, they calculated, the British could assemble in the port of Halifax, Nova Scotia, a fleet of 14 battleships, 38 cruisers, 5 aircraft carriers, 130 destroyers, and 34 submarines. Along with this armada, they figured 148,000 British troops would muster in Canada, supplemented with troops from India, Australia, New Zealand, South Africa, and even the Irish Free State, for a total of 2.5 million men.

With a force this size, in addition to Britain's navy and aerial might, Britain could quickly and easily invade the United States. The only reasonable defense, planners concluded, was a good offense: a rapid counterinvasion of Canada. Hence War Plan Red.

The American scheme, allegedly sketched out in its first draft in a matter of two hours, is an eerie mirror image of Brown's Defence Scheme No. 1, with invasions along almost identical paths as imagined by the Canadian lieutenant colonel. Its goal was nothing less than "the expulsion of Red [Great Britain] from North and South America ... and the definite elimination of Red as a strong competitor in foreign trade."

The first step was a naval takeover of Halifax, to deny the port as a staging area for the British. Moving north from Albany and Vermont, an armored column would take Montreal and Québec. From Detroit, another column would take Toronto, and from Buffalo, Niagara Falls, crippling the Canadian power grid. Grand Forks, North Dakota, would be the launch point for an invasion of Winnipeg, and, finally, from Bellingham, Washington, American troops would overpower Vancouver. These troop movement plans were devised with the help of transatlantic flight hero, and later Nazi sympathizer, Charles Lindbergh, who flew covertly as a spy to the west shore of Hudson Bay to investigate the possibility of using seaplanes for warfare and seek out points of low resistance as potential bridgeheads. He recommended the bombing of industries in Canada and the use of chemical weapons, supposedly outlawed by the Geneva Protocol of 1925.

The planners anticipated a war of "long duration" because "the RED race" is "more or less phlegmatic" but "noted for its ability to fight to a finish." Also, the British could be reinforced by "colored" troops from their colonies: "Some of the colored races however come of good fighting stock, and, under white leadership, can be made into very efficient troops."

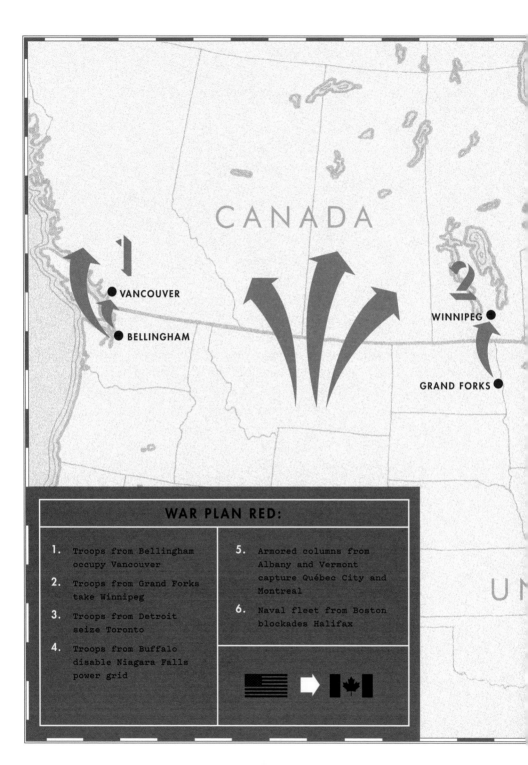

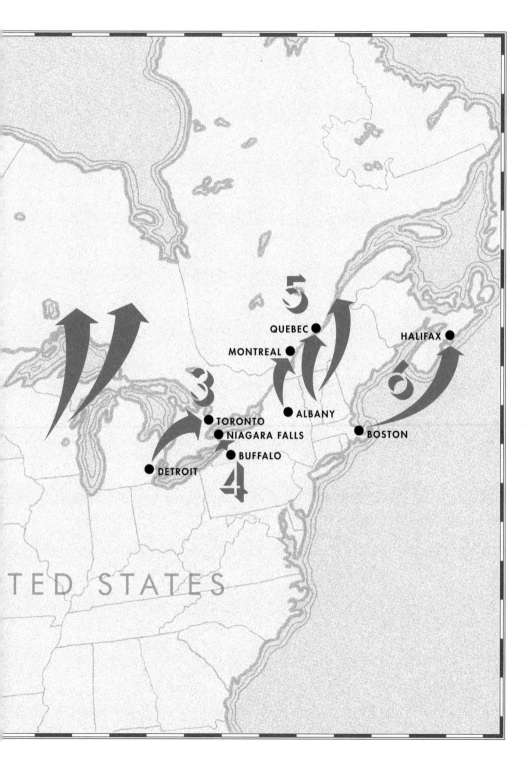

War Plan Red anticipated all sorts of problems, warning, for example, that the RCMP (Royal Canadian Mounted Police) is a fighting force not to be underestimated, and addressed the French (and, by extension, Catholic) question by asserting, "If the United States ever conquered Canada, the dual language would be done away with at once and the Roman Catholic Church would have much less power and influence by one hundred fold."

The detailed assessment of Canada's geography, industrial assets, and military power concludes that "Crimson [Britain] cannot successfully defend her territory against the United States (Blue). She will probably concentrate on the defense of Halifax and the Montreal-Québec line in order to hold bases of operation for Red. Important secondary efforts will be made to defend her industrial area and critical points on her transcontinental railroad lines." In other words, in the event of an invasion of Canada, the States would surely gain the upper hand, with no intention of returning the captured territory: "The policy will be to prepare the provinces and territories of CRIMSON and RED to become states and territories of the BLUE union upon the declaration of peace." And, QED, Canada would become part of the United States of North America.

Unlike Defence Scheme No. 1, War Plan Red found advocates outside the planning room, and, aided by the wildly unsuccessful Geneva Naval Conference of 1927—disarmament talks in which Britain insisted on twice the number of cruisers as America—the US Congress approved $57 million in February 1935 for an updated version of the plan. This money was also used to build three military airfields disguised as civilian airports on the Canadian border, which would be used to launch preemptive strikes against Canadian air forces and defenses. Simultaneously, the largest tactical war games in US history to that point, involving 36,500 soldiers, were staged at Fort Drum, only a grenade lob away from the Canadian border. The existence of these airfields was meant to be top secret but was accidentally revealed in a Government Printing Office brochure and then picked up by the *New York Times* as a front page story on May 1, 1935.

Britain did not seem too fussed by the revelations, however, if they even read them, and did not draw up its own war plan to resist an American invasion of their North American territory. Indeed, it continued to view Canada as indefensible against a much larger and more powerful United States, as it had for decades. Besides, the loss of Canada would not be a fatal blow to Great Britain, whose empire then covered about 25 percent of the world's landmass. As so often was the case, America was talking out of both sides of its mouth: just three years after authorizing an update to War Plan Red, President Franklin Roosevelt accepted an honorary degree at Queen's University, confirming that "The Dominion of Canada is part of the sisterhood of the British Empire. I give to you assurance that the people of the United States will not stand idly by if domination of Canadian soil is threatened by any other Empire." He continued, with a straight face, "We as good neighbors are true friends because we maintain our own rights with frankness, because we refuse to accept the twists of secret diplomacy."

In his address, Roosevelt warned already of "dangers from overseas," "wanton brutality, undemocratic regimentation, misery inflicted on helpless peoples, and violations of accepted individual rights," the winds of another global war that, only twelve months after his speech, would once again put the United States and Canada side by side, not sniping at each other across the border.

The full War Plan Red was not declassified until 1974, and unearthed, ironically, by Canadian journalist Robert Preston. The story was given more coverage by Peter Carlson, then a reporter for the *Washington Post*, when he asked John E. Taylor, a sixty-year veteran and head archivist of the National Archives in Washington, DC, what was "the weirdest document" he'd ever seen, to which Taylor immediately replied, "War Plan Red," the top secret document detailing how America planned to defeat its longtime frenemy, Great Britain.

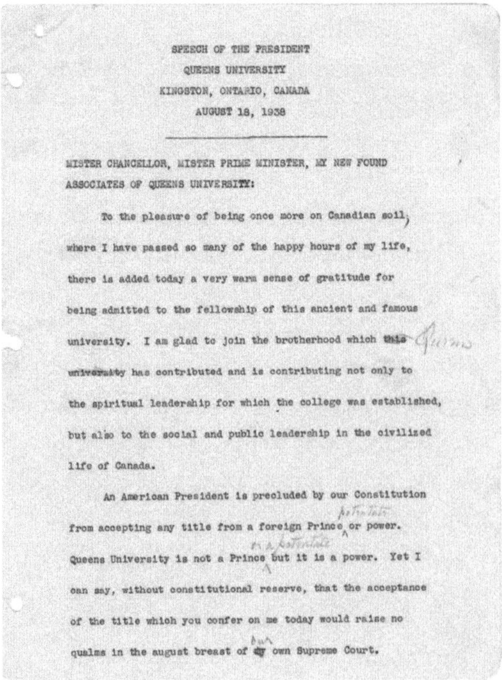

SPEECH OF THE PRESIDENT
QUEENS UNIVERSITY
KINGSTON, ONTARIO, CANADA
AUGUST 18, 1938

MISTER CHANCELLOR, MISTER PRIME MINISTER, MY NEW FOUND ASSOCIATES OF QUEENS UNIVERSITY:

To the pleasure of being once more on Canadian soil, where I have passed so many of the happy hours of my life, there is added today a very warm sense of gratitude for being admitted to the fellowship of this ancient and famous university. I am glad to join the brotherhood which this university has contributed and is contributing not only to the spiritual leadership for which the college was established, but also to the social and public leadership in the civilized life of Canada.

An American President is precluded by our Constitution from accepting any title from a foreign Prince or power. Queens University is not a Prince but it is a power. Yet I can say, without constitutional reserve, that the acceptance of the title which you confer on me today would raise no qualms in the august breast of my own Supreme Court.

Fig.27: Reading copy of President Roosevelt's August 18, 1938, address at Queen's University

WAR PLAN RUMSFELD

What Russia and the Cold War couldn't do—give the United States more or less de facto control over the Canadian military—Al Qaeda did.

With the end of World War II and the beginning of the Cold War, joining NORAD (North American Aerospace Defense Command), to sit inside the American "Sky Shield" and behind its twenty-five-ton blast doors beneath the Cheyenne Mountains at NORAD HQ, made tremendous political and strategic sense. It was a reflection of the postwar reality that Canada had become a possible nuclear target or, at least, likely collateral damage in an all-out bombfest between the United States and the Soviet Union. In a nod to Canadian sovereignty, and its oversized contribution to World War II (one million Canadians served, out of a population of eleven million, and Canada quickly conjured up the world's fourth-largest air fleet and fifth-largest navy), at least one of the two NORAD commanding officers is Canadian.

In April 2002, following the 9/11 terrorist attacks, President George W. Bush approved the creation of NORTHCOM (United States Northern Command) to "conduct operations to deter, prevent, and defeat threats and aggression aimed at the United States, its territories, and interests" over the entire North American region, including the contiguous United States, Alaska, Mexico, the Bahamas, the US Virgin Islands, and, of course, Canada. Curiously, Hawaii didn't make the cut, even pre-Obama.

Fully operational in October 2002, and headquartered at Peterson Air Force Base in Colorado Springs, Colorado, NORTHCOM has unilateral jurisdiction "to respond to [land

Fig.28: Canadian World War II propaganda poster

and sea] threats and attacks, and other major emergencies in Canada or the United States," boasted then Defense Secretary Donald Rumsfeld.

Canadian Prime Minister Jean Chrétien, having politely declined the opportunity to send Canadian troops into Iraq, refused to join NORTHCOM, but agreed instead to participate in a "Binational Planning Group (BPG)" to create "a neighborhood watch or collective security arrangement." Canadian critics worried this would eventually end up integrating the military command structures of the two countries by adding land and sea to the existing aerospace cooperation already covered by NORAD since 1957, fears that proved well-founded when the BPG morphed in 2006 into an expansion of NORAD to include "maritime domain awareness."

After effectively taking control of the Canadian military with his NORTHCOM initiative, Bush initiated the Security and Prosperity Partnership of North America (SPP) to cement further the mutual business interests of both countries. CNN journalist Lou Dobbs even speculated that SPP was a covert plan to merge Canada and the United States into a European Union–like entity, the North American Union. Dobbs went so far as to suggest that Bush would declare a state of emergency to keep himself in office. President Barack Obama, who also disapproved of NAFTA, a similar cross-border trade agreement, did not back SPP, and strong opposition in both countries caused it to be canceled in August 2009, but not until the expansion of NORAD's powers created the effect desired by the Bush/Rumsfeld regime.

Fig.29: Twenty-six-ton blast doors protecting NORAD headquarters deep beneath the Cheyenne Mountains

ANOTHER SURRENDER WITHOUT A SHOT

n the long tradition of battles won without a shot fired, World War II, the Cold War, and the so-called "War on Terror" ended 150 years of border tensions between the United States and Canada, making an invasion by either side, for military purposes, at least, no longer necessary. In fact, the establishment of NORAD after World War II already effectively accomplished an American invasion of Canada's military and de facto absorption of Canada into the American military-industrial complex.

The American television and entertainment industries rounded out the cultural aspects of the invasion, with many reciprocal imports from the north. But more than anything, commerce is the invasionary force that neither Buster Brown nor America's war planners foresaw: the Canadian and American economies are now so inextricably linked—each is the other's largest trading partner—that the invasion took place when nobody was really looking. If American TV, movies, and music mounted their own electronic invasion, Canadians have mounted their own counterinvasion force of citizen-soldiers:

- One in ten Canadians, more than three million, live full- or part-time in the United States, including 350,000 Canadians who work every day in New York City in the financial, media, arts, legal, and advertising businesses, making it Canada's fifteenth-largest city (see chart)
- More than one million Americans live in Canada.
- The seven hundred thousand First Nations Native Americans living in Canada have both US and Canadian citizenship, as

stipulated by the 1794 Jay Treaty, making them the equivalent population of the state of Alaska, by way of comparison.

- Fifty-nine million trips were made across the border in 2009 alone by citizens of both countries (two-thirds by Canadians heading south, one-third by Americans going north).

- Seventy-four percent of Canadian exports were sold to the United States in 2012, and 51 percent of its imports purchased from the States. Total American trade with Canada is actually larger than with China ($617 billion compared to $536 billion), and far more balanced (a deficit of $32 billion compared to a deficit of $315 billion).

Canada's Most Populous Cities

1.	Toronto, Ontario	5.58 million
2.	Montreal, Québec	3.82 million
3.	Vancouver, British Columbia	2.31 million
4.	Ottawa, Ontario	1.24 million
5.	Calgary, Alberta	1.21 million
6.	Edmonton, Alberta	1.16 million
7.	Québec City, Québec	766,000
8.	Winnipeg, Manitoba	730,000
9.	Hamilton, Ontario	721,000
10.	Kitchener, Ontario	477,000
11.	London, Ontario	475,000
12.	St. Catharines, Ontario	392,000
13.	Halifax, Nova Scotia	390,000
14.	Oshawa, Ontario	356,000
15.	New York, New York	350,000

1-14: Data from 2011 Census, Statistics Canada, www12.statcan.gc.ca/census-recensement/2011/dp-pd/hlt-fst/pd-pl/Table-Tableau.cfm?T=205&s=3&RPP=50
15: Data from Francis (2013)

The idea of a North American Union—first proposed by Henry Clay (who suggested Canada be taken by force) and picked up by Canadian Prime Minister William MacKenzie after World War II (who preferred to petition the American government, including a request for personal safe haven in the event of a future war)—is alive and well, even if rendered somewhat moot by the level of military and economic integration already in place: a 2005 document made available through WikiLeaks details an American government memo outlining the best strategy for a "North American Initiative," urging an incremental approach that would be an easier sell in Canada. Most recently, in 2013, respected journalist Diane Francis argued in her meticulously detailed and thoughtful book *Merger of the Century* that Canada and America should become one country, or, at least, a European Union–style union, with benefits to both: America gets access to Canada's natural resources and wealth, while Canada doubles the size of its economy and wins military protection for its long and vulnerable coastline. Among other threats, Francis worries about Vladimir Putin, who planted a titanium flag fourteen thousand feet below the North Pole (incredibly, neither personally nor bare-chested), claiming, "The Arctic is Russian!" Defending the Arctic coast at the moment is a volunteer militia: the Canadian Rangers, 4,400 part-timers with aging Enfield rifles, the same model Canadians used in World War I, and presumably the weapon of choice for Defence Scheme No. 1.

WAR AHEAD?

The Pentagon refuses to confirm that it maintains and updates plans for a military invasion of Canada as part of its ongoing program of war games and contingency planning. But there are several hard-to-ignore benefits a modern-day invasion of Canada would bring, so it's difficult to imagine that a twenty-first-century War Plan Red doesn't exist in a file folder there somewhere:

- Canada has the world's second-largest reserve of crude oil, after Saudi Arabia.
- Canada has about 20 percent of the world's fresh water supply (third after Brazil and Russia), which many believe will be the cause of our next global war.
- Canada has a functioning health care system and a longer life expectancy and lower infant mortality than the United States, not to mention lower rates of cancer, stroke, and heart disease.
- Canada is the sixth happiest country in the world, according to the 2013 World Happiness report issued by Columbia University, while the United States lags far behind at number seventeen.
- Assuming the Northwest Passage continues to melt due to global warming, Canada will soon be the gatekeeper of the American continent's largest transverse waterway, and maybe the only one if the Panama Canal is closed by terrorists, an unfriendly government, or lack of maintenance.

What the United States has to offer in the event of a Canadian invasion is much less clear, however, so, being the more sanguine of the neighbors, it's likely that Canada has not iterated Defence Scheme No. 1, if the only spoils would be:

- Miles of warm southern beaches (many already frequented by Canadian "snowbirds"; Canadians are the largest "foreign" real estate holders in America, accounting for 24 percent of such sales in 2011).
- Repatriation of some of Canada's most famous and creative citizens who've moved south, including 250,000 in Hollywood alone, behind or in front of the camera (from Seth Rogen to William Shatner), and numerous celebrated musicians, such as Neil Young, Bryan Adams, Joni Mitchell, and Justin Bieber. The recovered tax revenues would be substantial.
- An overabundance of embarrassing politicians, so if a future Rob Ford needs to be hidden in a room of his ilk, America is the place to blend him in.
- Important hockey-related reasons: the Zamboni company is headquartered in Paramount, California, and a takeover of the United States would guarantee that the Stanley Cup is housed permanently in Canada.

For better or worse, the United States also has much more recent combat experience than Canada. Though much of that has been sand- rather than snow-based, the American military is well-armed and equipped, and, in spite of calls for a smaller army, is, in fact, at its largest ever, with more than five hundred thousand troops. Canada has total military personnel of 119,000, of which only 68,000 are on active duty. Any armed conflict between the countries would be tremendously lopsided, even though Canada has a history, as we've seen, of beating the odds when stacked against them. Given the comingling of finances, it seems most likely that a "war" between the two nations would be a cyber or financial one, with freezing of assets, unplugging of cell phone or ATM networks, and other nonviolent passive-aggressive tactics more likely to bring civilians to their knees than cutting off mail service to Maine in 1812, and then bringing Canada into the union. Happily, this seems both unlikely and unnecessary, since the war is, in effect, behind us and not ahead. Our two countries have slipped quietly into peace, in spite of Defence Scheme No. 1, War Plan Red, and centuries of border tensions, a far better blueprint for neighboring nations than any invasion scheme.

The benefits of union and denials of invasion aside, there are signs that the spirit of War Plan Red lives on. In 1969, the United States sent a turbocharged icebreaker, the USS *Manhattan*, through the Northwest Passage, waters Canada had claimed only a few months earlier as sovereign territory. The timing was hardly coincidental: the US State Department warned, "We cannot accept the assertion of a Canadian claim that the Arctic waters are internal waters of Canada.... Such acceptance would jeopardize the freedom of navigation essential for United States naval activities worldwide." The United States conceded, in 1985, that future trips by American icebreakers "would be with the consent of the Government of Canada. It's hard not to hear in this the sneer of a bully: we'll warn you because we don't think you can do anything about it. And even some in the US government aren't convinced by Obama's claim that there is no modern-day War Plan Red. During a Senate Appropriations Defense Subcommittee hearing on June, 18, 2014, Senator Dan Coats (R-IN) said that, based on his knowledge, "the Pentagon has a contingency plan on the shelf for just about every possible scenario," including "an invasion by Canada."

DEPARTMENT OF MILITIA AND DEFENCE.

WAR LETTER No. 1.   Ottawa, April 11th, 1921.

I am directed to forward herewith, Copy
of Defence Scheme No.1. (United States).

Chapter number 2, will follow within the
course of a few days. Succeeding chapters will
follow at early dates. These instructions will
precede any other communications for defence
purposes concerning the United States.

Your attention is particularly called to the
note on the top of Chapter No.1, re secrecy. It is
to be particularly noted that there are matters of
this nature, and that no one is to be informed
about except yourself.

Steps are to be immediately taken to work out
your plans for, 1, Mobilisation, 2, for Training
War, 3, for Operations of War as directed by
the Defence Scheme,

Chapter 1 and succeeding chapters will call
for Reports, Local Schemes, Lists of Staffs, Recommendations, etc. I will consider all these matters
and do not call them in as the last chapter
will call definitely for the Reports, etc. that you
will have to send in, and it will be suggested in
that chapter the form that these Reports, etc. will
take.

The names of higher commanders left blank in
the Scheme, will be communicated secretly to you
later on.

                    Colonel,
              Director of Military Operations and
                    Intelligence,
              for Chief of the General Staff.

APPENDIX A

WAR PLAN RED

A UNITED STATES PLAN FOR INVASION OF CANADA

The following is a full-text reproduction of the updated
plan for a US invasion of Canada prepared at the US Army War
College, G-2 intelligence division, and submitted
on December 18, 1935. This is the most recent declassified
invasion plan available from US archival sources.
The spelling and punctuation of the original document
are reproduced faithfully, except for true errors, which
have been silently corrected.

SUPPLEMENT NO. 3
TO
REPORT OF COMMITTEE NO. 8
SUBJECT:
CRITICAL AREAS OF CANADA AND APPROACHES THERETO

Prepared by:
SUBCOMMITTEE NO. 3

Major Charles H. Jones, Infantry, Chairman.
Lt. Col. H.W. Crawford, Engineers.

I. Papers Accompanying
1. Bibliography.   (Omitted, filed in Rec. Sec.)
2. List of Slides.   "
3. Appendices (1 and 2).   "
4. Annexes. (Incl. A,B,C,D,E,F,G,H,K, and L) "

II. The Study Presented.
Determine under the geographical factor, the critical
areas in Crimson (Canada) and the best approaches thereto
for Blue. A critical area is assumed to be any area
of such strategic importance to either belligerent that
control thereof may have a material bearing on the outcome
of the war.

III. Facts bearing on the study
1. General Considerations:
An area in Crimson territory may be of strategic importance
from the viewpoint of tactical, economic, or political
considerations. In the final analysis, however, critical
areas must be largely determined in the light of Red's
probable line of action and Crimson's contribution to
that effort.
2. Geographical Features of Canada.
   a. Location and extent.
   The location and extent of the Dominion of Canada is
   shown on the Map herewith (see Exhibit A). It comprises
   the entire northern half of the the North American
   continent, excepting only Alaska and the coast of
   Labrador, a dependency of the colony of Newfoundland.

The principal political subdivisions are those located
along the border of the United States. These, from
east to west, are:

   (1) The Maritime Provinces:

   Prince Edward Island.

   Nova Scotia.

   New Brunswick.

   (2) Québec.

   (3) Ontario.

   (4) The Prairie Provinces:

   Manitoba.

   Saskatchewan.

   Alberta.

   (5) British Columbia.

   Newfoundland, while not a part of the Dominion
   of Canada, would undoubtedly collaborate in any
   Crimson effort.

b. Topography. (Slide 14852)

The great area in eastern Canada underlain by rocks
of Precambrian age is known as the Canadian Shield.
Its northern boundary crosses the Arctic archipelago;
the eastern boundary lies beyond Baffin Island and
Labrador, and reaches the depressed area occupied by the
St. Lawrence, a short spur crossing this valley east
of Lake Ontario to join the Adirondack Mountains of New
York. The southern boundary runs from this spur west
to Georgian Bay thence along the north shore of Lake
Huron and Lake Superior, thence northwest from the Lake
of the Woods to the western end of Lake Athabaska.
Its average elevation does not exceed 1500 feet. The
greatest known elevations are in the eastern part of
Baffin Island and along the coast of northern Labrador.
Peaks of the Torngat Mountains of Labrador have
elevations of between 4000 and 5000 feet. The coast is
one of the boldest and most rugged in the world, with
many vertical cliffs rising 1000 to 2000 feet high.
Occasional exceptions occur in which there are reliefs
of several hundred feet, as in the hills along the
north shore of Lake Huron and Lake Superior. The area
is dotted with lakes, large and small, and of irregular

outline. A lowland of considerable extent stretches for
some distance into Ontario and Manitoba from Hudson
Bay. Extending south and west from the Canadian Shield,
between the Appalachian Mountains on the east and the
Cordilleras on the west, lies the Great North American
plain. The northeastern portion of this plain called the
St. Lawrence lowlands occupies southern Ontario, south
of a line extending from Georgian Bay to the east end of
Lake Ontario; eastern Ontario lying between the Ottawa
and St. Lawrence rivers, and that part of Québec lying
adjacent to the St. Lawrence between Montreal and
Québec. The plain west of the Canadian Shield, known as
the Interior Plains, stretches northward to the Arctic
Ocean between a line approximately joining Lake Winnipeg
and Lake Athabasca,Great Slave Lake and Great Bear Lake
on the east, and the foothills of the Rocky Mountains on
the west. That part of the St. Lawrence Lowlands lying
in the eastern angle of Ontario, and in Québec south
of Montreal and extending down the St. Lawrence is
comparatively flat and lies less than 500 feet above sea
level. On the lower St. Lawrence it is greatly narrowed
by the near approach of the Appalachian system to
the Canadian Shield. The part lying adjacent to Lakes
Ontario, Erie and Huron is of less even surface, has its
greatest elevation of over 1700 feet south of Georgian
Bay and slopes gently to the Great Lakes. The Interior
Plains region is in general rolling country with broad
undulations and a slope eastward and northward of a
few feet per mile, descending from an elevation of 3000
to 5000 feet near the mountains on the west to less than
1000 feet at the eastern border. The rolling character
of the area is relieved by several flat topped hills, by
flat areas that formed the beds of extensive lakes, and
by deep river valleys. The Appalachian and Arcadian
regions occupy practically all that part of Canada lying
east of the St. Lawrence, with the exception of the
lowlands west of a line joining Québec City and Lake
Champlain. The Appalachian region is a continuation into
Québec of three chains of the Appalachian system of
mountains. The most westerly of these ranges, the Green

Mountains of Vermont, stretches northeast into the
Gaspe peninsula, where it forms flat topped hills some
3000 feet high. The Acadian region, which includes New
Brunswick, Nova Scotia, and Prince Edward Island, is
an alternation of upland with hills and ridges rising
2500 feet and higher. Adjacent to the Bay of Fundy is
a series of ridges rising in places to 1200 feet.
Between these two New Brunswick uplands, which converge
toward the southwest is a lowland forming the whole
eastern part of the province. This lowland extends east
to include Prince Edward Island, the western fringe of
Cape Breton Island and the mainland of Nova Scotia north
of the Cobequid mountains, which have an elevation of
800 to 1000 feet. South of the Cobequid Mountains lies
a long narrow lowland stretching from Chedabucto Bay to
Minas Basin, and along the Cornwallis Annapolis valley
between North and South Mountains. South of this lowland
is a highland sloping to the Atlantic Coast. The
northern part of Cape Breton Island is a tableland
1200 feet high with its central part rising to an
elevation of over 1700 feet.
The Cordilleran region, a mountainous area bordering
the Pacific extends from the United States through
Canada into Alaska and embraces nearly all of British
Columbia and Yukon and the western edge of Alberta
and the Northwest Territories. The eastern part of the
Cordillera is occupied by the Rocky Mountains, with
peaks rising to 10,000 feet and 12,000 feet. They extend
northwest and fall away towards the Liard River. The
western part of the Cordillera is occupied by the Coast
Range and the mountains of Vancouver and Queen Charlotte
Islands. The Coast Range rises to heights of 7000
to 9000 feet. Between the Rocky Mountains and the Coast
Range lies a vast plateau 3000 to 4000 feet high and
cut by deep river valleys.

3. Population.

According to the census of 1931, the total population
on June 1, 1931 was 10,376,786, of whom 5,374,541 were
males. The inhabited areas of the Dominion are essentially
confined to a narrow strip along the United States boundary,

generally south of the 56th parallel of latitude west of
the Lake Winnipeg, and south of the 49th parallel of
latitude east of Lake Superior. Approximately 10% of the
total population are found in the Maritime provinces, 61%
in Québec and Ontario, 23% in the Prairie Provinces and
6% in British Columbia. Of the present population, 51.86%
are of British descent, 28.22% French, and the remainder of
widely scattered nativity.

4. Climate.

The climate of southern Canada is comparable to that of the
northern tier of the states of the United States. The west
coast of British Columbia tempered by the Pacific Ocean is
mild and humid. The prairie provinces generally experience
extreme cold weather from November to March, with heavy snow
fall. The climate of southern Ontario, the St. Lawrence
Valley and the Maritime Provinces is much milder than that
of the prairie provinces, but freezing temperatures are
general between the end of November and the first of April,
and the ground is usually covered with between one and three
feet of snow. Any extensive military operations in Canada
between November 1st and April 15th would be extremely
difficult, if not impossible.

5. Communications.

    a. Railways.

There are only two railway systems in Canada, both
crossing Canada east and west from the Atlantic to the
Pacific. These lines generally parallel the United
States border, in some instances crossing through the
United States.

        (1) The Canadian national Railways system (See
inclosure B) belonging to and operated by the
government, has eastern terminals at Halifax, N.S.,
Portland, Maine (Grand Trunk), and through Central
Vermont, at Boston, New London and New York. Western
terminals are Vancouver and Prince Rupert B.C.
An extension from Cochrane, Ontario, to Moosonee,
Ontario on James Bay, was completed by the Province
of Ontario in July 1932, to connect with water
routes to Churchill, Hudson Bay and with the northern
route to Europe.

(2) The Canadian Pacific system (see inclosure C) has its eastern terminus at Saint John, N.B. and it western terminus at Vancouver, B.C. As indicated by the systems maps, there are numerous branch lines serving the industrial and farming areas of the Dominion, and connecting lines tying in with various railroads of the United States. From a military viewpoint, these railroads provide excellent transportation facilities for Blue, if invasion of Crimson is decided upon, and being located in close proximity to the border are, from the Crimson viewpoint, very liable to interruption. This is particularly true at Winnipeg some 60 miles north of Blue's border, through which both transcontinental systems now pass. This fact probably encouraged Canada to construct the railroad from The Pass, Manitoba and develop the port at Churchill. Complete details concerning all railroads of Canada are contained in Appendix No. 1.

b. Highways.

In recent years Canada has greatly increased and improved her road construction and while there are enormous stretches of country, particularly in the northern portion of the Dominion, with few or no roads, the southern portion is well-served with improved roads. A number of transcontinental motor roads are under construction or projected, the most important being the "Kings International Highway" from Montreal to Vancouver, via Ottawa, North Bay, Sudbury, Sault Ste. Marie, Winnipeg, MacLeod, Crow's Nest Pass, Fernia and Cranbrook. Another highway is being constructed from Calgary to Vancouver. The principal roads in Ontario, Québec and the Maritime Provinces are shown on Inclosure D, herewith. Roads in the Prairie Provinces and British Columbia are shown on inclosure E. The majority of improved roads are classified as gravel; macadam and concrete construction amounting to only 7870 miles out of a total of some 95,000 miles improved. Gravel roads will require extensive maintenance under heavy motor traffic, especially during the spring.

c. Water Transportation.

(1) Inland Waterways.

The Great Lakes, with the St. Lawrence River, is the most important fresh water transportation system in the world. At the present time it affords a draft of 21.0 feet over all the Great Lakes and through the Welland Canal into the St. Lawrence. From the Atlantic Ocean to Montreal, the present head of ocean navigation on the St. Lawrence, a draft of 30.0 feet is available, adequate for the great majority of ocean shipping. For some distance above Montreal the present channel has an available depth of only 14.0 feet.

The inland waterway is of prime importance to the economic life of both the United States and Canada for the transportation of bulk commodities, especially for the movement of wheat from the western plains to shipping centers on the eastern seaboard; of iron ore from the mines in Minnesota to foundries along Lake Ontario; and for coal from the mines of Pennsylvania and West Virginia to Ontario, Québec and the northwest.

The locks at Sault Ste. Marie, the boundary channels between Port Huron and Detroit and to a lesser degree the Welland Canal are the critical points on this waterway and effective control of such areas is vital to Blue.

Navigation on the Great Lakes is generally closed by ice from about the end of November to the first of April.

The St. Lawrence River is ordinarily ice bound for a similar period, but somewhat later about early in December to the latter part of April. While there are a number of Canadian lake ports of importance, Montreal is the only one which would not be automatically closed by Blue control of the Lakes. Montreal is also an important ocean port and will be considered along with other deep sea ports.

(2) Ocean Shipping.

The Dominion of Canada owns and operates a cargo and

passenger carrying fleet consisting of some 57 cargo
vessels and 11 passenger ships. The principal ocean
ports and the magnitude of Canadian ocean traffic is
indicated by the following tabulation:

(a) Number and tonnage of sea-going vessels
entered and cleared at the principal ports
of Canada.

(For year ending March 31, 1934.)

SEA-GOING VESSELS

PORT	arrived	departed	TOTAL TONS (REGISTERED)
Halifax, N.S.*	1259	1484	7,540,990
Yarmouth, N.S.	535	519	1,102,191
St. John, N.B.*	684	688	2,924,822
Montreal, Québec*	1078	907	7,266,569
Québec, Que.*	397	308	3,388,829
Prince Rupert, B.C.	1141	1155	251,881
Vancouver, B.C.*	2332	2137	11,705,775
Victoria, B.C.	1927	1938	8,874,481
New Westminster, B.C.	678	700	3,123,606

IMPORTANT SECONDARY PORTS

Churchill, Man.*	15	15	132,000
Three Rivers, Que.	79	79	424,560
Windsor, N.S.	56	69	201,032

Note: The above figures do not indicate amount
of commerce; Register tons are gross tons.
(Namely cubical contents in cubic feet divided
by 100) less deductions for crews space,
stores, etc.
A brief description of the above ports to
indicate size, available depths and important
terminal facilities is included in Appendix
No. 2. While the above tabulation lists
the principal ports, it should be realized that
there are a large number of less desirable ports
having available depths at low water of 20 to
30 feet and provided with satisfactory terminal

facilities, which can be used in an emergency
for landing troops or supplies. Examples of
this class of harbors are:

    Pictou, N.S.

    Sydney, N.S.

    Canso, N.S.

    Gaspe, Québec

    Sorel, Québec

The port of Montreal, favorably located at the
head of ocean navigation on the St. Lawrence and
the foot of inland navigation of the Great Lakes,
is a natural shipping and railroad center.
The port of Québec is less favorably situated
economically being more than 100 miles northeast
of Montreal. Strategically, however, Québec
controls the commerce of Canada moving to or from
the Atlantic seaboard. Its possession by Blue
would interrupt eastern rail and water
communication between England and the Maritime
Provinces and the rest of Canada. The port of
Halifax is one of the best harbors on the
Atlantic Coast and the principal winter port of
Eastern Canada. The harbor has been extensively
developed by the Dominion government as a
modern ocean terminal and naval base. It is
fortified, though much of the armament is
obsolescent. In case of war with Red, Halifax
would become of prime importance to Red as
a naval base and as a debarkationpoint for
overseas expeditions in case Blue controlled the
St. Lawrence. However, the routes available
for a Red advance from Halifax into northeastern
United States or towards Québec and Montreal are
quite difficult. The port of Saint John, New
Brunswick is similar in manyrespects to the
port of Halifax. It is open throughout the year
and equipped with the most modern terminal
facilities, including one of the largest dry-
docks in the world. It is an important shipping
center for grain and dairy products. Due to the

proximity of the port to the United States
border and the fact that the principal rail
connections (C.P. Ry.) pass through the state
of Maine, the port would be of little use to
Crimson or Red, at least in the early stages of
war, provided Blue made any effort to control
this area. The port of Vancouver, B.C. came into
prominence with the opening of the Panama Canal,
providing an alternate route to that of the
transcontinental railroads for grain, dairy,
lumber and the other products of western Canada
to Europe. The port of Victoria, on Vancouver
Island, is similarly situated, but due to the
absence of rail connection with the mainland is
more concerned with passenger and mail traffic
than with bulk commodities. Esquimalt, two miles
west of Victoria, and the only Canadian naval
base on the west coast, is equipped with a large
modern dry-dock, and affords good anchorage for
the largest vessels. Consequently this area is of
prime importance to Crimson. With the closing of
the Panama Canal to Red traffic and the presence
of Blue naval forces based on Honolulu, its
commercial value is largely destroyed. Assuming
that Blue controls the St. Lawrence and
cuts Crimson's eastern communication with Red,
the area's importance is enhanced, although it
remains a decidedly unsatisfactory outlet. If Red
should win control of the Pacific steamship
lanes, the area becomes of first importance to
Red. All factors considered, it must be
controlled by Blue. The port of Prince Rupert is
a first class harbor with modern terminal
facilities and excellent and extensive
anchorages. It becomes of extreme importance to
Crimson, if and when they are denied the use
of the southwest British Columbia ports,
although, as in the case of Vancouver, it affords
a most unsatisfactory and hazardous route to
Europe. Physical occupation of Prince Rupert

harbor by Blue is not vital, but closing the port
to ocean traffic should be effected. The port of
Churchill, Manitoba now offers a good harbor
and limited but modern terminal facilities,
affording a back door to the Prairie Provinces
and, by way of Moosonee, Ontario, and the
Temiskaming and Northern Ontario Railroad, with
central and western Ontario. Hudson Bay and James
Bay are open to navigation only about 4 months of
the year, but this condition is partially offset
by the fact that the distance from the Prairie
Provinces to Europe, via Churchill is from 500 to
1000 miles shorter than the rail-water route via
Montreal. In case Red is denied the use of the
Atlantic or Pacific ports, or both, Churchill
will afford an outlet for grain and meat products
from Ontario, Manitoba and Saskatchewan and an
inlet for military supplies and troops from
Europe unless the northern trade route through
Hudson Strait is controlled by the Blue fleet,
and this is improbable.

d. Air Transportation (Civil).
During 1933 there were 90 commercial aircraft
operators in Canada. Their activities included forest
fire patrols, timber cruising, air photography,
transportation of passengers, express and mail, etc.
To encourage a more widespread interest and knowledge
of aviation the Department of National Defense, since
1928, has issued two light airplanes and made certain
grants to each of 23 flying clubs and a large air
terminal has been built at St. Hubert, seven miles south
of Montreal and a terminal airdrome at Rimouski, Québec
for the reception of trans-atlantic mails. At the
close of 1934 there were 101 air fields of all types,
368 civil aircraft and 684 licensed pilots in Canada.
Some details of airports in New Brunswick and Nova
Scotia are given in a letter from the Office of
the Chief of Air Corps, herewith. (See inclosure F)
e. Telephone and Telegraph.
    (1) Cables.

Six transoceanic cables have termini in Canada, five
on the Atlantic and one on the Pacific. The Atlantic
cables are landed at Halifax, though several of them
are routed through Newfoundland. The Pacific cable
lands at Vancouver from whence a cable also leads
to the United States.

(2) Radio.

A transoceanic commercial radio beam service is
carried on by a station at Drummondville, Québec,
with Australia, Great Britain and the United States.
In 1932 a direct radio telephone circuit with
Great Britain was opened through the medium of
this beam station.

(3) General.

Canada is well-supplied with local telephone,
telegraph and radio service. Interruption of Canada's
trans-oceanic telegraph and radio service will
seriously handicap Red-Crimson cooperation.

6. Other Economic Factors.

a. Agriculture.

Agriculture, including stock raising and horticulture,
is the chief single industry of the Canadian people.
Canada is not only self-sustaining, as far as food
is concerned, but has a large excess for export. Food
production is varied and so distributed throughout
the dominion that each section is practically self-
sustaining and cutting her off from the outside would
mere serve to deny her people certain luxuries, such
as coffee, tea, sugar, spices and tropical fruit.
The Maritime Provinces are noted for their fruit and
vegetable crop, particularly for the oat and potato
crops of Prince Edward Island and New Brunswick
and apples in Nova Scotia. Québec and Ontario are
mixed farming communities with the Niagara peninsula
specializing in fruit. Manitoba, Saskatchewan and
Alberta are the principal wheat producing centers, with
other grains and stock raising of increasing importance.
The rich valleys of British Columbia produce apples,
other fruit and vegetables.

b. Forests.

The principal forests are in the provinces of British
Columbia, Ontario, Québec, New Brunswick and Nova
Scotia. The manufacture of lumber, lath, shingles and
other products such as paper pulp, is the second most
important Canadian industry.

c. Mineral Resources.

Canada is one of the greatest mineral-producing
countries of the world. Nova Scotia, British Columbia,
Québec, Ontario, Alberta and the Yukon Territory contain
the chief mining districts. The following summary notes
pertinent facts concerning minerals of primary military
importance. Aluminum. Aluminum was the 16th ranking
Canadian export in 1934. Large quantities of bauxite,
the principal source of supply were imported from
the United States. Coal. There are enormous deposits
of coal in Canada, largely in Nova Scotia and New
Brunswick, in the east and in Alberta, Saskatchewan and
British Columbia in the west. Due mainly to the distance
of the fields from the manufacturing and industrial
centers, about 50% of the coal consumed is imported from
the United States, via the Great Lakes. Statistics for
the calendar year 1933 show:

Produced:

Nova Scotia	6,340,790	tons
New Brunswick	314,681	"
Manitoba	3,036	"
Saskatchewan	903,776	"
Alberta	4,748,074	"
British Columbia	1,484,653	"
Yukon Territory	638	"

Imported:

From United States	8,865,935	tons
From United Kingdom	1,942,875	"
Total	22,265,235	tons.

(see slide 14855)

In case of war with the United States, Canada's
coal imports from this country would be cut off and
her railroads and industrial activities seriously
handicapped. If Blue controlled the Québec area and

Winnipeg, Canada's railroads and industries dependent
upon "steam power" would be crippled.

(1) Copper.

The world production of copper in 1933 was
(in short tons):

Canada	149,992
Mexico	43,900
Rhodesia	144,954
Peru	28,000
Belgian Congo	73,409
Spain and Portgual	34,720
Chile	179,200
Japan	75,459
United States	196,190

Canada's production was distributed approximately
as follows:

Province	Tons	
Québec	35,000	Eastern Townships
Ontario	72,700	Sudbury area
Manitoba	19,000	Flin Flon
Saskatchewan	1,600	
British Columbia	21,600	Western Manitoba

(2) Iron and Steel.

Canada ranks seventh among the nations as a producer
of iron and steel but only a small percentage
of her production is derived from domestic ores,
in view of the abundant supply of higher grade
ores in Newfoundland and Minnesota. The Wabana
section of Newfoundland contains the largest known
single deposit of iron ore in the world. There are
large iron ore deposits in Québec, northern Ontario
and British Columbia but for various reasons they
are handicapped for blast furnace treatment. Iron
and steel are produced in Nova Scotia (Sydney)
and in Ontario. Iron ore is obtained from the Mesabi
Range in Minnesota, via the Great Lakes and from
Newfoundland. (See slide 14856) The bulk of iron and

steel products, however, are imported, principally
from the United States and the United Kingdom.
(3) Lead.
Lead is obtained in Canada largely from deposits in
British Columbia, the largest portion being exported
to England.
(4) Nickel.
The world production of nickel in 1933 was about
50,736 tons, of which about 82% originated in the
Sudbury district, north of Georgian Bay in Ontario.
The remainder came chiefly from New Caledonia (Fr.).
A new deposit of nickel was recently discovered
in northern Saskatchewan but has not yet been worked.
Nickel is necessary to industry and indispensable
in war. Control of the Sudbury mines, in case of war,
is therefore of vital importance.
(5) Petroleum.
The production of crude oil or petroleum in
Canada during 1934 amounted to 1,417,368 barrels,
principally from the Turner Valley field in Alberta.
A small amount is also obtained from wells near
Monkton, New Brunswick and in southwest Ontario,
between Lake Huron and Lake Erie. Considerable
quantities are also imported from the United States.
(6) Zinc.
Canada ranks fourth among the worlds producers of
zinc. Her output in 1934 totaled 298,579,531 pounds.
The principal producing mines are located in the
Kootenay district of British Columbia and near Flin-
Flon in northwest Manitoba. Approximately 2/3 of
the zinc exported goes to Great Britain.
d. Manufacturing.
(1) General.
Canada is the second largest manufacturing country
in the British Empire, with Ontario and Québec
the most important industrial centers. The relative
standing of the various provinces during 1933,
based on the value of products manufactured, was
approximately as follows:

Ontario	$1,000,000,000.
Québec	650,000,000.
British Columbia*	146,500,000.
Manitoba	91,000,000.
Alberta	55,000,000.
Nova Scotia	53,000,000.
New Brunswick	45,000,000.
Saskatchewan	36,000,000.
Prince Edward Island	3,000,000.

*Includes Yukon Territory

The principal industries ranked according to gross value of products (1932) are:

Pulp and Paper	$123,415,492.
Central Electrical Stations	117,532,081.
Non-ferrous metal smelting	100,561,297.
Slaughtering and meat packing	92,366,137.
Flour and food mills	83,322,099.
Butter and Cheese	80,395,887.
Petroleum Products	70,268,265.
Bread and other bakery product	51,244,162.
Cotton yarn and cloth	51,197,628.
Printing and publishing	50,811,968.
Clothing factory, women's	44,535,823.
Automobiles	42,885,643.
Rubber goods	41,511,556.
Hosiery and knitted goods	40,997,210.
Sawmills	39,438,057.

(2) Munitions.

(a) Aircraft.

There are at present six firms manufacturing aircraft as follows:

Canadian-Vickers.......Montreal, Que.
De Haviland...........Toronto, Ont.
Curtis Reid...........Cartierville, Que.
Fairchild.............Longueuil, Que.
Boeing................Vancouver, B.C.
Ottawa Car Mfg. Co.....Ottawa, Que.

Aero engine factories have been established by:
Armstrong-Siddeley Motors Co. at Ottawa, Que.
Aero Engines of Canada at Montreal, Que. Canadian
Pratt-Whitney Aircraft Co. at Longueuil, Que.
(b) Miscellaneous.
During the World War Canada demonstrated her
ability to divert her peace time industries
to the production of munitions, when she
manufactured and exported large quantities
of shells, fuses, cartridge cases, explosives,
gun forgings, machine guns and small arms
ammunition. This production could not be obtained
in case of war with Blue but some munitions
could be produced if her factories were free to
operate and raw materials were available. The
government arsenal at Lindsey, Ont., is equipped
to produce small arms ammunition and the arsenal
at Québec manufactures some small arms and
artillery ammunition.

e. Commerce.
Analysis of Canada's industry and resources indicate
that she has a sufficiency or surplus of certain raw
materials but a deficiency of others. The more important
of these materials are as follows:
(1) Sufficiency or surplus; Arsenic, asbestos,
cadmium, cobalt, copper, feldspar, fish oil,
fluorspar, foodstuffs, furs, gold, graphite, gypsum,
lead, leather, magnesium, mica, nickel, silver, talc,
wood and zinc.
(2) Deficiency; Aluminum, antimony, bauxite, barytes,
camphor, chromite, coal, cotton, flax, hemp,
iron, jute, kaolin, manganese, mercury, nitrates,
phosphate, petroleum, opium, quinine, rubber, silk,
sugar, sulphur, tea, tin, tobacco and wool.

7. Combat Estimate.
a. All matters pertaining to the defense of Canada
are under a Department of National Defense (Act of Jan.
9, 1923) with a minister of National Defense at the
head. A Defense Council has been constituted to advise
the Minister.

b. The Navy has an authorized complement of 104 officers and 812 men, a large majority serving under 7 year enlistments. In addition certain specialists are loaned from the British Royal Navy. The Reserve consists of from 70 to 113 officers and from 430 to 1026 men recruited from sea-faring personnel. The ships of the Royal Canadian Navy are:

Built	Class	Displacement	Name	Location	Status	Armament
1931	Destroyer	1337 tons	Saguenay	Halifax, N.S.	In commission	4-4.7"
1931	"	137 tons	Skenna	Esquimalt, B.C.	"	4-4.7"
1919	"	905	Champlain	Halifax, N.S.	"	3-4"
1919	"	905	Vancouver	Esquimalt, B.C.	"	3-4"
1918	Mine Sweeper	360	Armentieres	Esquimalt, B.C.	"	
1918	Mine Sweeper	360	Festubert	Halifax, N.S.	In reserve	
1918	"	360	Ypres	Halifax, N.S.	"	

c. Army.
    (1) Personnel: Estimated Strength (by G-2):

Organized Forces.

	Active	Reserve	Total
Permanent Active Militia	403		403
Officers	403		403
Men	3,300		3,300
Non Permanent Active Militia			
Officers		6,911	6,911
Men		44,962	44,962
Reserves, Non-active			
Officers		10,000	10,000
Men		30,000	30,000
Total Organized	3,703	91,873	95,576*

Note: The Canada Year Book, 1935, pp 1114, gives permanent and non-permanent active militia 1934:

    Permanent Officers and men-------- 3,760
    Non-permanent officers and men---- 135,184
                  Total 138,941

The latest information concerning the distribution of the active militia is shown on the accompanying map. (Incl. G)

(2) It is probable that the Non-permanent Active Militia can be brought to a strength of 60,000 at M plus 15 and to full strength of 126,000 in M plus 30 days. (Note: This estimate is approximately twice that of G-2, First Army.) New troops will begin to appear in 180 days at the rate of 50,000 monthly.

d. Air Service. The Royal Canadian Air Force operates under a directorate in the office of the Chief of Staff of the Army.

Strength (Dec. 1, 1934)

Active:	
Officers	117
Men	664
Reserve:	
Officers	38
Men	236
Total	1,055

The equipment consists of some 84 combat planes with probably 20 on order. (G-2 estimate) The Armaments Year Book, League of Nations, gives a total of 166 planes of all kinds and the Statesman Year Book, 1935 gives 189 planes of all kinds. It is probable that about one squadron of pursuit and one squadron of observation could be organized for immediate service.

e. Comment.

The location of Canada's industry and population along a narrow extent front facing the northern United States border and her relatively weak military and naval forces, widely dispersed, will necessitate a defensive role until Red forces are landed. The promptness and effectiveness of British aid must depend upon suitable debarkation points on Canada's east coast. The West Coast does not favor overseas operations unless Red controls the Pacific, and even then is too remote from critical Blue areas.

f. Red Reinforcements.

Various estimates have been made of the size, composition, and time of placing Red reinforcements in Canada. In any such estimate, the time factor is of prime importance but depends on an unknown quantity, viz, "the period of strained relations." The following estimate is considered conservative:

Probable Enemy Forces in Canada

Days after M Day	Crimson Men	Div.	(Less Crimson) Men	Location Div.	Men	Total Divisions
15	25,000	5			25,000	5
30	50,000	5			50,000	5
60	50,000	5	126,000*	8	176,000	13
90	50,000	5	203,000	13	253,000	13
120	50,000	5	238,000	16	288,000	21
150	50,000	5	255,000	16	305,000	21
180	90,000	5	255,000	16	345,000	22

*Under certain conditions this force might be landed in Canada by 30 M.

Air Forces.

Red has available at once 48 squadrons of 10 to 12 planes each. The following forces can probably be landed in Canada as indicated.

10M	13 squadrons.
30M	30 squadrons.
60M	41 squadrons.
90M	56 squadrons.
120M	74 squadrons.

g. Conclusion.

Crimson cannot successfully defend her territory against the United States (Blue). She will probably concentrate on the defense of Halifax and the Montreal-Québec line in order to hold bases of operation for Red. Important secondary efforts will be made to defend her industrial area and critical points on her transcontinental railroad lines.

8. Areas of Strategic Importance. Analysis of the above data and discussion indicates certain areas which would become of considerable military importance in the event of war with Red; namely,

a. The Halifax Monkton St. John area, sometimes called the Martime Province area.

b. The Montreal Québec area, sometimes called the St. Lawrence Area.

c. The Great Lakes Area.

(1) Niagara River Area.

(2) Sarnia-Windsor Area.

(3) Sault Ste. Marie Area.

(4) Sudbury Area.

d. Winnipeg Area.

(1) Winnipeg City and vicinity.

(2) Churchill, Manitoba Area.

e. Vancouver-Victoria Area.

(1) Ports of Vancouver and Victoria, area.

(2) Prince Rupert area.

f. The reasons why these various areas are strategically important may be briefly summarized as follows:

(1) Halifax Monkton St. John Area.
(Maritime Province).
The port of Halifax is the key point in the area, for while the port of St. John affords excellent facilities for an overseas expedition, it is so close to the United States border that uninterrupted use by Red cannot be expected. At Monkton, the peninsula connecting Nova Scotia and the mainland narrows to 14 miles. With Halifax in possession of Crimson, this area affords the best defensive position to prevent any advance westward by Red.

(a) Control of Halifax by Blue would:

1. Deny Red the only ice free port on the east coast and the only ports, other than the St. Lawrence River ports, suitable as an overseas base.

2. Deny Red a prepared naval base on the east coast, from which to operate against Blue naval forces or commercial shipping.

3. Disrupt transoceanic submarine
cable service between Crimson and Red (except
from Newfoundland) and between Crimson and
the West Indies.
4. Deny Red the use of certain air bases
from which to operate against northeastern
United States.
(b) The control of Halifax by Blue, renders
the Port of St. John and the Monkton area of
secondary importance. Failing to secure Halifax
control of the Monkton area by Blue would:
1. Deny Red the use of St. John Harbor.
2. Cut the lines of communication between
the port of Halifax and St. John and the
remainder of Canada.
3. Place Blue directly across the only line
of advance (by Red) from Halifax, on the
shortest possible defensive line.
4. Deny Red the use of certain air bases
from which to operate against northeastern
United States.
5. Give Blue the use of various small air
fields at Monkton and St. John.
(2) Montreal Québec Area (St. Lawrence River Area).
The ports of Montreal and Québec, while ice bound
about four months of the year, still afford the best
overseas base both as to facilities and location. In
addition the area is of great commercial importance
in that it controls all lines of communication, by
land, sea and wire between industrial and agricultural centers of Canada and the eastern seaboard.
While Montreal has the larger and more commodius
harbor and terminal facilities, Québec, due to its
physical location, is the key point of the area.
(a) Control of this area by Blue would:
1. Deny the use of all good St. Lawrence
River ports to Red.
2. Cut all Canada, west of Québec, viz.
industrial, and agricultural centers from the
eastern seaboard.

3. Deny Red and Crimson and make
available to Blue, the principal air bases
in eastern Canada.
4. Deny Crimson coal and iron from Nova
Scotia and Newfoundland as well as all
imports via the Atlantic.
(3) The Great Lakes Area.
This area comprises several critical points:
(a) Niagara River crossings and Welland Canal.
(b) The waters connecting Lake Huron and
Lake Erie.
(c) The great industrial area of Canada–that
part of Ontario lying between Lake Huron and
Lakes Erie and Ontario.
(d) The waters connecting Lake Superior and Lake
Huron, including the Soo Locks.
(e) The Sudbury nickel-copper mines.
Control of the Great Lakes waterway is vital
to Blue, for the transportation of iron ore,
coal and grain and such control will necessitate
occupation of a bridgehead covering the narrow
boundary waters at and near the Soo Locks and
in the Detroit Area. The bridges over the Niagara
River and the Welland Canal, connecting Lake Erie
and Lake Ontario are of importance to Blue for
occupation of the Important industrial area
of the Niagara-Ontario peninsula. The Welland
Canal would become of importance as a line
of communication if Blue seized the peninsula.
While control of that area is of importance
in crippling Crimson industry, it is probably
of greater importance in denying the enemy
Crimson and Red, a most convenient base for
operations against highly industrialized areas
in the United States.
(4) Winnipeg Area.
Winnipeg is the nerve center of the transcontinental
railroad system. Control by Blue will effectively
separate eastern and western Canada and block
transportation of men, grain, coal, meat and oil to

the east. The completion of the Canadian National
Railroad to Churchill Manitoba on Hudson Bay and
the development of the port at Churchill provide an
alternate route to Europe via Moosonee, Ont., and
the Tem. and Ont. Ry. to northeast Ontario. While the
water route through Hudson Bay is only open about
four months of the year, and the ports are supplied
by single track railroads, a considerable amount of
traffic could be developed in an emergency.

(5) Vancouver Victoria Area. As pointed out above,
the ports in this area are of secondary importance
only under the conditions, which may reasonably
be assumed. However, the area has certain military
importance, due to the naval base at Esquimalt, and
is a possible outlet for the Canadian plan provinces
and western Canada. Its control by Blue would deny
the enemy any base or outlet on the West Coast;
simplify the problem of protecting our shipping in
the Puget Sound area; and interrupt cable communication with the far east. While Prince Rupert, B.C.
has an excellent harbor and terminal facilities with
good rail connections leading east, naval blockade
of this port would be readily possible, once the
Vancouver Victoria area was in Blue control.

9. Routes of Approach to the Areas of Strategic Importance.
a. Halifax Monkton St. John Area (Maritime Provinces)
(Incls. D & H). Three possible routes of approach are
considered, viz:

(1) Via water from Boston or New York to Halifax
or vicinity.

(2) Via water from Boston or New York to ports in
Western Nova Scotia and thence overland to Halifax.

(3) From Eastern Maine, via St. John and/or
Fredericton to Monkton Amherst Truro to Halifax.

b. Discussion of Routes of Approach to the Halifax
Monkton St. John (Maritime Province) Area.

(1) The distance by water from Boston to Halifax
is 370 miles and from New York 600 miles, or in
time about 30 or 50 hours respectively. The Port of
Halifax is fortified and would undoubtedly be mined.

A frontal attack would require a large force and would involve undesirable delays. Other developed ports of Nova Scotia on the Atlantic are too distant from Halifax and involve a long advance after a landing is effected and this advance would be over difficult terrain.

A number of undeveloped bays along the east shore offer favorable conditions for landing operations and of these, St. Margarets Bay, the nearest, being some 16 miles by road west of Halifax, appears satisfactory. Deep water, with a minimum depth of 7 fathoms extends nearly to the head of the Bay, not far from Hubley and French Village, which are on an improved road and on the railroad from Yarmouth to Halifax. The bay is protected from all winds and seas, except those from the south and is of sufficient size to harbor any fleet required for the expedition. Tidal range is the same as at Halifax, 6 to 6 1/2 feet. There are numerous small but adequate boat and barge landings on the west, north and east shore of the bay, from whence improved roads lead to the main highway.

The highway Hubbard French Village Hubley Halifax is 18 feet wide, of macadam, with east grades and with concrete bridges capable of carrying heavy artillery and tanks. The railroad is single track, standard gauge and parallels the road. It has rather heavy grades and is of light construction.

Rocky wooded hills rise rather steeply to a height of 200 to 400 feet all around St. Margarets Bay, but the roads are within the 50 foot contour and the terrain between the roads and the water is greatly rolling. The main highway French Village Halifax, runs through low rocky hills and movement off the roads by wheeled vehicles would be practically impossible.

(2) The ports on the western shore of Nova Scotia off the Bay of Fundy are subjected to extremely high tides 20 to 25 feet, and generally afford only limited terminal facilities and have depths generally inadequate for docking transports. Tidal currents are

strong. From Windsor, on the Avon River, to Halifax, there is one improved road and a branch of the Canadian Northern Railroad. The distance is about 50 miles, with high ground and good defensive positions in the center of the island. As a route of approach to Halifax it is considered inferior to the route from St. Margarets Bay.

(3) The All-Land Route via Eastern Maine.

This route involves an advance from the Maine border of approximately 320 miles over difficult terrain. The St. Johns River, rising near the border of northern Maine, flows south just east of the Maine New Brunswick border to Woodstock, thence generally southeast through Fredericton to St. John. It is navigable from the mouth to the falls some distance above Woodstock, N.B. The average tidal range at St. John is 20 1/2 feet, decreasing up stream. The river is crossed by a highway and a railroad bridge at Fredericton, each nearly 1/2 mile long. Two other bridges, a cantilever railroad bridge and a suspension bridge span the river about one mile above the city of St. John. There are numerous ferries operating alone the river. It is apparent that the St. John River is a serious obstacle to any advance overland from Maine. While the St. John could be bridged, such operations would result in considerable delay. The railroad and road nets available are shown on Enclosures B, C and D. They are reasonably adequate for a force of the size probably required for this operation.

(4) Conclusion.

If Halifax is to be captured without the use of large forces and expenditure of considerable time and effort, it must be accomplished promptly before Red reinforcements can be landed or Crimson organize for its defense. Any advance overland from Maine would eliminate all elements of surprise and make the capture extremely difficult—a major operation.

An overseas expedition is one of the most uncertain of military operations, and with the Red fleet on guard in the North Atlantic, with Red's immediate military objective the retention of a base in eastern Canada for future operations against Blue, a joint operation against Halifax must be promptly and perfectly executed to assure any hope of success. This route is considered the best but existing conditions at the time, may make this route impracticable, and the all land route necessary.

c. The St. Lawrence Area. (Québec Montreal) The only practicable routes of advance for Blue, into this area, are from northern New York, New Hampshire and Vermont and from northwest Maine. (See map) (Incl. K)

(1) Rivers.

(a) The St. Lawrence River flanks the left side of all routes of approach to Québec. From Montreal to Three Rivers it flows through an alluvial plain, with the south bank 25 to 75 feet above the river. Below Three Rivers the banks increase steadily in height to Québec, where they are 140 to 175 feet high. The normal rise and fall of the river above the tidewater is 10 feet but this maybe doubled by ice jams. Tidal range reaches a maximum of 18 feet at Québec, and practically disappears at Richelieu Rapids 40 miles above Québec. The river above Québec is obstructed by ice from November to April but ice breakers can get through. The river from Québec to Montreal, generally about 1/2 to 2 miles wide (except at Lake St. Peter) is navigable on a 30' draft to Montreal. The distance from Québec to Montreal is 160 miles. In the area south of the St. Lawrence, between Québec and Montreal, are several rivers of importance which will naturally influence any plans for an advance on Québec, viz:

Richelieu River
St. Francis River
Nicolet River
Becancour River
Chaudiere River
Etchemin River

Other streams will create obstacles of lesser
importance.

(b) The Richelieu River flows north from Lake
Champlain to enter the St. Lawrence about 35
miles north of Montreal. It is navigable on a
6 1/2 foot draft throughout its length.

(c) The St. Francis River rises in St. Francis
Lake some 50 miles northwest of Jackman, Maine.
It flows southwest to Lennoxville, Québec,
where it turns sharply northwest to flow into
the St. Lawrence (Lake St. Peter). Headwaters
are controlled. The regulated flow is some
3000 feet per second or more, with an average
fall of 6.6 feet per mile. It is not fordable
below Sherbrooke.

(d) The Nicolet River rises in Nicolet Lake,
8 miles west of Lake Alymer, and flows generally
northwest to empty into the St. Lawrence at the
east end of Lake St. Peter. The average low water
flow is about 2000 feet per second. Banks in
the upper reaches-hilly wooded terrain-are steep
and from 200 to 500 feet higher. The average fall
is about 21 feet per mile but there are a number
of dams. From Arthabaska to Lake St. Peter the
stream flows through a flat open country, with
banks 25 feet high or less, except for a gorge
starting about 4 miles north of St. Clothilda and
ending 3 miles from Lake St. Peter. The river is
not a serious obstacle but there are many swampy
areas between it and the Becancour River.

(e) The Becancour River rises about 5 miles
northwest of Lake St. Francis and flows north,
then southwest, then northwest to enter the St.
Lawrence a few miles below Three Rivers, Que.
The lower reaches of the river, below the
vicinity of Lyster, Que., flows through generally
flat country of gentle slope. The stream averages
300 to 400 feet wide and is fordable at few
places. From Maddington Falls to within 3 miles
of the St. Lawrence the river flows through

a narrow gorge 100 to 250 feet below the
surrounding flat country. The river is not
a serious obstacle to an advance on Québec, by
reason of the general direction of flow in
its lower reaches and the characteristics of
the country.

(f) The Chaudiere River rises in Lake Megantic,
about 45 miles west of Jackman, Maine and flows
generally north into the St. Lawrence, opposite
Québec. From Lake Megantic to Hersey Mills,
it flows swiftly between steep banks in a
narrow valley. The adjacent terrain is rugged
and heavily timbered. From St. George to Valley
Junction the valley widens materially and the
country is less rugged. Below Valley Junction
the river flows through gentle undulating country
between relatively low banks. The Chaudiere is a
strong swift stream with an average discharge
of over 4000 feet per second. The width varies
from 200 feet at St. George to 400 feet or more
in the lower reaches. From St. Maxine to the
St. Lawrence it is 600 to 1500 feet wide. This
river must be considered a serious obstacle.

(g) The Etchemin River rises in Lake Etchemin and
flows northwest into the Chaudiere. It is 200 to
300 feet wide in the lower reaches, with
banks generally high and steep. It forms a
considerable obstacle.

(2) Terrain.

The southerly portion of the area bordering on the
United States, east of the Richelieu River, is hilly
verging on mountainous (up to 3000'). The Notre Dame
Mountains extend the Green Mountains of Vermont in
the form of a series of ridges, gradually decreasing
in elevation from Lake Champlain northeast to the
meridian of Québec, thence northeast parallel to the
St. Lawrence. From the St. Lawrence the terrain rises
smoothly and gradually toward the southeast to the
foothills of the Notre Dame Mountains. On the line
Montreal Sherbrooke a serious of eight hills (wooded)

rise sharply to heights varying from 800 to 1500 feet
or more above the surrounding country. In general the
hills of the Québec theatre are wooded, those below
the 500 foot contour and east of the Becancour River
sparsely, while west of the river there are densely
forested areas at intervals.

(3) Roads.

The main roads to Montreal lead north from
Plattsburgh, New York and Burlington, Vermont.
Québec may be reached via routes No. 1 and 5, through
Sherbrooke, Que; via route No. 3 along the south bank
of the St. Lawrence; or via Montreal and the north
bank of the St. Lawrence. The latter is the longest
route and undoubtedly the most difficult. Another
route is available from Jackman, Maine, via route
No. 23 through Valley Junction. The road net
available is shown on inclosure No. "D" and "K."

(4) Railroads.

The railroads available are shown on inclosures "B"
and "C." They are entirely adequate for any probable
movement against this area.

(5) Discussion of routes.

   (a) Northern New York Vermont to Montreal Roads:
   No. 9 from Plattsburgh to St. Lambert and South
   Montreal. Distance 69.2 miles, all paved.
   No. 7 from Burlington, Vt., via St. John, Que.
   to St. Lambert or South Montreal. Distance
   94.2 miles, all paved. There is a bridge across
   the Richelieu River at St. Johns. There are
   two highway bridges across the St. Lawrence
   at Montreal.
   Railroads: Delaware and Hudson Albany to
             Montreal.
             New York Central Malone to Montreal.
             Rutland and C.P. Burlington to
             Montreal.
             Central Vermont and C.N. Montpelier to
             Montreal.
   Comments: The terrain is favorable and no
   physical barrier to the advance as far as the

St. Lawrence, except the crossing of the
Richelieu River, for a force moving from Vermont.
An advance on Québec from Montreal is possible,
but offers the longest route, with many
rivers perpendicular to the line of advance
(down the St. Lawrence) which offer excellent
defensive positions.

(b) Northern Vermont and New Hampshire to Québec.
Physical features: The Richelieu River on the
west and the Chaudiere and Etchemin Rivers
on the east tend to delimit the zone of advance.
Roads: No. 5 Newport, Vt. to Sherbrook then No.
7 to Valley Junction to the highway bridge on the
St. Lawrence and to Québec, or via No. 23 from
Scott Junction to Levis, Que. and the ferry
to Québec. Distance 212.5 miles from Newport,
Vt. All improved road, mostly gravel. Some of the
road through the hilly country is paved. No. 5
from Sherbrooke via Victoriaville is an alternate
route. No. 23, Jackman, Maine Valley Junction
Levis. This distance is 109 miles. The road is
improved and about 50% paved. It is the shortest
route. It crosses the Chaudiere and Etchemin
Rivers. There are numerous alternate routes and
connecting roads.

Railroads:

Canadian Pacific Newport to Québec.
Canadian Pacific Jackman via Megantic to Québec.
Canadian National Portland, Me., via Sherbrooke
to (c) Québec.

Comments: While the terrain in this sector
is hilly verging on the mountainous, with several
defiles and river crossings, it offers the
shortest and best route of advance on Québec.

d. The Great Lakes Area.

This area must be considered under the following
subdivisions, as the routes of approach vary, and
approach must be made from all of these directions.
The Buffalo Niagara River Area.
The Port Huron Detroit Area.

The Sault St. Marie or Soo Locks Sudbury Area.

(1) The Buffalo Niagara River Area. Bridges cross the Niagara River at Buffalo (Peace Bridge); at Niagara Falls (suspension Bridge) and the (lower Arch Bridge) and at Lewiston, New York.

Roads: The road net approaching the Niagara River from the United States and leading across the river into southern Ontario and through Hamilton to Toronto and Montreal, is one of the best along the international boundary and is entirely adequate for any probable movement.

Railroads: The Canadian Pacific and the Canadian National railroads have a network of railways connecting Buffalo with Toronto and points east. Branch lines lead to all important parts of the Niagara peninsula. Comment: The crossings over the Niagara River should be promptly secured to assure a line of advance into the Niagara Peninsula of Ontario.

(2) The Detroit Port Huron Area. This area has much the same characteristics as the Buffalo Niagara River Area but beyond securing the crossings over the boundary waters, sufficient area to cover the Great Lakes water routes against Crimson interference is essential.

Crossings: Ambassador Bridge Detroit-Windsor. Two tunnels (one railroad) Detroit-Windsor. Numerous ferries. Railroads and roads: There is an excellent railroad and road net available for any advance eastward from Detroit and Port Huron. Comment: The Ontario Peninsula is of great industrial importance to Canada and a military area of great strategic value, as a base for air or land operations against the industrialized areas between Chicago and Buffalo. Any Blue operations should advance via Buffalo Niagara Falls and Port Huron Detroit simultaneously.

(3) Sault Ste. Marie Sudbury Area. The best route of approach to the Sudbury area, about 200 miles east of the Soo, is obviously via Sault St. Marie, along the

north shore of North Channel. An operation along this
route, automatically covers the Soo. The Canadian
Pacific railroad and one good gravel road leads east
from the Soo. These provide ample facilities for
supply of the probable force required. The southern
flank of this line is protected by North Sound
and the north flank by rough heavily wooded terrain
entirely devoid of roads or other communications
suitable for the movement of armed forces.
(4) Winnipeg Area. The main route from the United
States to Winnipeg is north from Grand Forks and
Crookston through Emerson. A main road follows
the west bank of the Red River, from Emerson into
Winnipeg. A good hard surface road from Grand Forks
and one from Crookston furnishes a suitable road
net south of the border. There are several secondary
roads on both sides of the border to supplement the
hard surface roads. The Canadian Pacific has two main
lines extending north from the border, one leading
from Fargo through Gretna along the west bank of
the Red River, and one from Thief River Falls,
through Emerson along the east bank of the Red River.
The Canadian Northern has a line from Grand Forks
through Emerson Junction to Winnipeg on the west bank
of the Red River and another line connecting with
Duluth and extending through Warroad to Winnipeg.
The best and only practicable route of approach
is obviously north from Grand Forks and Crookston.
The terrain is flat and open and offers no natural
obstacles to an advance. Churchill, on Hudson
Bay, has rail connection by the Canadian National
system at Hudson Bay Junction about 325 miles
northwest of Winnipeg. The best and only route of
approach to cut this line is along the railroad
from Winnipeg.
(5) The Vancouver Area (Vancouver Victoria) (See
Incl. E & L) (Omitted) The best practicable route
to Vancouver is via Route 99 through Bellingham,
a distance of 55 miles and over a paved highway,
through wooded and farming country. A secondary

and longer route lies about 15 miles further to the east running through Sumas to strike the highways running east from Vancouver at the meridian of Mission City. The Grand Trunk Railroad extending from Vancouver to Seattle furnishes a satisfactory rail service. Victoria and Esquimalt, on the island of Vancouver can be reached by water only. Ferry service is maintained between Vancouver and Nanaimo on the east shore of the island, some 50 miles north of Victoria and between Vancouver, Burlingham and Port Angeles and Victoria. The best route of approach is by water from Port Angeles, Washington.

IV. Conclusions:

    a. That the critical areas of Canada are:

        (1) The Halifax-Monkton-St. John Area (The Maritime Provinces).

        (2) The St. Lawrence Area (Québec and Montreal).

        (3) The Great Lakes Area.

        (4) The Winnipeg Area.

        (5) The Vancouver Area (Vancouver and Victoria).

    b. That the best routes of approach to these areas are: To

        (1) By joint operations by sea from Boston.

        (2) From Northern New Hampshire-Vermont area.

        (3) (a) From Sault St. Marie and the Soo Locks Area.

            (b) From Port Huron Detroit Area.

            (c) From the Buffalo-Niagara Falls Area.

        (4) From Grand Forks-Crookston through Emerson.

        (5) Along Puget Sound through Everett and Bellingham, supported by an attack by water in Puget Sound.

V. Recommendations

None.

VI. Concurrences.

The committee concurs in the foregoing conclusions.

CHARLES H. JONES Major, Infantry,

Subcommittee Chairman.

APPENDIX B

Extracts from

DEFENCE SCHEME NO. 1

DEFENCE OF CANADA - GENERALLY

Section 1. Problems to be met by the Empire

The Imperial General Staff is of the opinion that the
possible eventualities, which the Empire must be prepared
to meet, fall roughly under two main headings:
1. A struggle for the existence of the Empire such as that
from which we have only recently emerged.
2. Minor crises which may be only local in character but
which may synchronise or spread until a situation develops
straining the resources of the Empire very greatly without
enabling us to take the extreme methods which would be
justified by a great national emergency.

These latter cases would probably call for the employment of
the full authorised Forces of the Crown in the various parts
of the Empire, namely, Regular Army and Permanent Forces;
territorial forces and militia forces, to be kept
up to strength by voluntary enlistment, but would not
call for national service in the case of other parts of
the Empire or Levee en Masse in the case of Canada.
The major eventuality is a plain straightforward issue, but
it is considered by the Imperial General Staff that it could
scarcely arise without the inclusion of one of the great
civilised powers in the enemy's ranks. Although there are
indications that we may be faced by a hostile Russo-German
combination and signs of danger from other centres are
not absent, the British Cabinet has come to the conclusion
that a war similar to that which has just been concluded
is not likely to recur during the next 5 or 10 years.
The Imperial General Staff held at the same time that such
an eventuality cannot be lost sight of entirely, and though
neither the locality nor the chief actors can at present
be foretold, it will be wise to take such general measures
as will enhance the value of the Land Forces of the Empire
as a whole, without prohibitive expenditure, such as (a)
the co-ordination of military thought throughout the Empire,
including measures for ensuring the close co-operation
of Staffs, which was so marked a feature of the recent

struggle, (b) the standardisation of establishments and
equipment, (c) the drawing up of schemes in each part
of the Empire for the distribution of man power as between
the three Services and the industries necessary to maintain
armies in the field with a view to obtaining the maximum
value for the available man power. From this it will be
possible to assess for different parts of the Empire the
relative proportion of effort to be devoted to each of
the three Services, which will best suit the requirements
of the Empire as a whole, (d) the extension in Peace time
and the expansion in War of industries intimately connected
with the supply of warlike material in order that Indian
and Dominion Forces may be, so far as possible, self-
supporting, (e) the distribution of responsibility for
the collection of intelligence and arrangements for
co-ordinating the results.
The above are matters which will be discussed at the
approaching Imperial Conference.
The Defence of Canada, therefore, falls under two
categories: -
1. Direct Defence, i.e., the immediate defence of our
country against invasion by hostile forces;
2. Indirect Defence, by which we send an Expeditionary Force
to bring the hostile country or countries to action in their
own country or countries, or in any case, in territory
beyond the confines of the Dominion of Canada.

Section 2. Three Defence Schemes Necessary

For a struggle for the existence of the Empire, it would
appear that four cases may occur:-
1. A European Combination
2. The United States
3. Japan
4. A combination of the above.
Only (2) and (4) of the above and possibly in a lesser
extent (3) would put Canada in immediate danger of invasion
and call for the Levee en Masse. It is necessary, therefore,
to draw up three different Defence Schemes: -
1. For the Defence of Canada against the United States.

2. For the Defence of Canada against Japan.
3. For the Organization and the Despatch of an Expeditionary
Force to help the Empire in case of a European Combination
or a Minor Crisis. . . .

Section 3. General Strategical Situation of Canada

The first thing apparent then in the defence of Canada is
that we lack depth.
Depth can only be gained by Offensive Action. To carry
out an Offensive Action against the United States, with our
population in a ratio of 1 to 12 and the United States'
Regular Army of 175,000 Enlisted Men, and with between
two and four millions of men who were lately embodied
for service, is a difficult and on the surface an almost
hopeless task, but on further study, it would be found out
that it is not as hopeless as it appears on the surface
and that Canada has a good many advantages in her favour.
To carry out an Offensive Action against the United States
means, first of all, Quicker Mobilisation; secondly, the
immediate despatch of Flying Columns on the declaration
of War; thirdly, the despatch of our Formations at Peace
Strength to be followed rapidly by drafts filling them to
War Establishment; fourth, a speedy mobilisation of our
Reserve Units by General Recruitment and by putting in force
the Levee en Masse, as soon as Proclamation is made; fifth,
the completion of the organisation of our Formations by
the inclusion of Reserve Units; sixth, the despatch of
Reserve Units to certain garrisons or certain strategical
points; seventh, the early formation of Depots.
Time is of the essence of everything of our mobilisation
and of our early operations. To keep up this offensive
and to continue the successful defence of Canada, will
require the timely arrival of reinforcements from the Empire
and particularly from the United Kingdom and the full use
of the man power and resources of the Empire in other
theatres of operation, namely, the Atlantic Seaboard of
the United States; the Southern Seaboard, i.e., the Gulf
of Mexico, Florida and Mexico; the Pacific Coast.
In order to carry out this Offensive, well chosen lines

of Offence should be decided upon, these to produce the
greatest results, firstly, to increase our Depth; secondly,
to increase our resources by the occupation of hostile
territory; thirdly, to increase the moral [sic] of our
population with a corresponding decrease of moral of the
enemy; fourthly, to cover the organisation and mobilisation
of our man power and to prevent the destruction of our
resources and lateral communications; fifthly, to gain
time until the arrival of help from the various parts of
the Empire, as soon as the man power and the resources
of the Empire are mobilised and transported to their various
spheres of action.

SEA POWER
Sea Power is another of the most important factors in the
Defence of Canada. To keep open for periods, at least,
the seas for the transport of Britannic and Imperial troops
to the various Theatres and for the protection of our
Atlantic and Pacific Coasts, to prevent our flanks from
being turned, to prevent our Ports of Disembarkation for
help from the Empire being occupied or destroyed.
Control of the Great Lakes
Another important strategical feature in the Defence of
Canada is the control of the Great Lakes. On all, except
Lake Ontario, the Americans have a preponderance of shipping
and they have in the States bordering the Great Lakes a
Naval Militia of considerable size, which could be made use
of to arm and man United States' Mercantile Great Lakes boats.
Timely arrival of British ships of suitable size in Lake
Ontario and the proper protection of the Welland Canal,
might ultimately give us control of Lake Erie.
Many Canadians, including many navigating officers, are
serving in the United States' Great Lakes Mercantile Marine.
Further information concerning this question will have to
be gathered and action taken to put their service into use
at the appointed hour.

WINTER CAMPAIGN
A winter campaign, for obvious reasons, by a large force, is

not feasible, but the subject should not be lost sight of, as we might be forced into a winter campaign and in any case mobilisation might have to take place during the winter and tactical raiding would be feasible.

POLITICAL QUESTIONS

1. Statesmen decide on the Time, Circumstances, and the Locality of War and leave it to the Soldier to make the best of them. It is hoped that our Statesmen will act in such a manner to give us as many advantages as possible in case war becomes inevitable between the British Empire and the United States of America. Members of Parliament and Members of the Senate are drawn from various sources of life, most of them with no War Service and very many of them with no militia connection and no knowledge of the vast machinery required for War and of the terrible disadvantage of loss of the initiative at the commencement of a campaign. It is your duty then to do what you can within your sphere of action to see that such political personages are enlightened on questions of Defence.

2. French Canadians (all Roman Catholics) form nearly one third of the population of Canada. They took little interest in the Great World War. There may have been "Vatican" influence, but it would appear that the main reason for lack of interest was lack of proper political control and leadership from Ottawa. The Roman Catholic Church in Canada is suspicious of the Militia. It has no reason to be so. It has everything to gain and nothing to lose by supporting the Militia. If the United States ever conquered Canada, the dual language would be done away with at once and the Roman Catholic Church would have much less power and influence by one hundred fold.

3. Americans in Canada. Many in British Columbia. Well over 50% in Alberta. Over 50% in Saskatchewan. Many others holding important positions, especially in manufactures and transportation, in other parts of the country.

4. Census, 1921. Commanders should obtain information from the Census, 1921, as soon as the Census Report is compiled, as it will give the latest information of foreign population and of man power of the various Commands and Districts.

5. Provincial Jealousies. Friendly rivalries between the
East and the West and between the various Provinces may
help to stimulate matters, but every care should be taken
to prevent Provincial or Parochial matters interfering
with broad questions. There is a tendency for Provincial
politicians to interfere with proper organisation and there
will probably be the same tendency to prevent the proper
distribution of troops in time of war. This tendency may
only be eliminated by education. . . .

Section 9: Allies or Possible Allies of Great Britain

Japan. Japan is still an Ally of Great Britain. The question
of the renewal of the Japanese Treaty comes up this year.
Whatever Japan's attitude may be at any other time, there is
not much doubt, in case of war between the British Empire
and the United States, that Japan would take immediate
military action against the American Republics, in which
case it would make matters much more favourable to us,
especially at the beginning of the campaign, if we would
find that Japan would carry out her traditional policy of
delivering their Declaration of War and a Military Operation
at the same time . . .
France. France has always taken a friendly interest in the
United States. She came to her help during the Revolutionary
War and for years the American Army organisation and tactics
were based on the French system. France has seen more in
the last two years of the modern "Yank". She is dissatisfied
with American action, with the low rate of exchange of the
franc in the United States, with the attitude of the United
States towards the League of Nations. It would appear then
that the United States would get no support either actively
or sympathetically from France.
Mexico. It has a turbulent and unruly population estimated
from 12 to 15 millions. For over 100 years it has been
a pin-prick on the American Southern Flank. The Mexicans
have not shown themselves, generally speaking, opposed to
British interests. In case of war with the United States
it is not unlikely that Mexico would cause trouble on
the Southern Frontier, causing a goodly force of United

States' troops to be concentrated towards Mexico. If Mexico became an active participant in a War against the United States, it would be an area of operation for Britannic or British Empire troops against the Southern States, having for its object the capture of Galveston and New Orleans, and blocking the Mississippi River.

The South American Republics. Many of whom are not hostile to British interests and might decide to support the British Empire. Many of these Republics possess Navies of a useful size which would be a tremendous factor in operations against the Panama Canal.

Section 10: The Strategic Importance of Newfoundland, Alaska and West Indies.

Alaska. The Alaskan Coast presents harbours to be used as submarine bases of operation against the British Columbian Coast. A sufficient force of regular troops might be kept on the Southern Alaskan Coast to capture Prince Rupert by a coup de main, immediately after the declaration of war.

Newfoundland. [Newfoundland] enters largely into the Defence of Canada. American occupation of the Island would have far reaching results. It would be on the flank of the sea routes between Great Britain and Canada and it would be a menace to all our shipping and a base for naval operations against Nova Scotia, the Gulf of the St. Lawrence, and the St. Lawrence River generally. Newfoundland would appear to be a rendezvous and a probable base of operations for the British Grand Fleet.

West Indies. The West Indies are admirably situated as bases for naval operations against the Southern States and particularly against the Panama Canal. They are situated on the flank of the Panama Canal route and if, by any chance, the United States' fleet or any great portion of it was in the Pacific at the outbreak of war the use of the Panama Canal for concentration on the Atlantic Coast might be denied absolutely to them.

CHAPTER TWO: PROBABLE ACTION OF THE UNITED STATES

Main Objectives.
The main objective of the United States force would
undoubtedly be Montreal and on to Ottawa. The next important
objective of the United States would be the occupation of
the Ontario Peninsula, including the cities of Hamilton and
Toronto. The other objectives at which the American Land
Forces would be moved against would be Québec, Winnipeg,
the Island of Vancouver and South Western British Columbia,
i.e., the area including Vancouver and New Westminster.
The grain growing Provinces of Manitoba, Saskatchewan,
and Alberta which now have a large percentage of Americans,
are especially attractive to the United States, and
there is just a possibility that they might make
the conquest of these Provinces the ultimate objective
of their campaign. . . .
First attempt Invasion of Canada – Mode of:
It is considered that the first attempt of the invasion
of Canada would take place as mentioned above by the
use of Flying Columns, to carry out a great strategical
stroke to catch us unawares before the Canadian Militia was
mobilised. If this was not successful, it is considered
that there would be a period elapsing of possibly a couple
of weeks before a determined effort would be made to advance
on Canada by Divisions of all Arms.
Organisation of Our Flying Columns for Immediate Action
This emphasises the fact that our Flying Columns must
be organised for immediate action: that our Divisions must
get underway with units at Peace Strength with the least
possible delay, that is, within three or four days of the
declaration of war. This is the object to work up to in
the Scheme for Mobilisation.
If, after careful study, and taking into consideration
the improvement that is sure to come in the position of
Militia recruiting, you consider that your units will not
be able to move towards their war station on the third
or fourth day of mobilisation, please advise the General
Staff at Ottawa of that fact and of what time you estimate
that your Division will be on the move to its War Station.

Section 2: General Instructions for Offensive Action

All training and organisation in Peace and all arrangements
during the Precautionary Period will lead up to a general
Limited Offensive against the United States.
Pacific Command. The field troops of the Pacific Command
to advance into and occupy the strategic points including
Spokane, Seattle, and Portland, Oregon, bounded by the
Columbia River.
Prairie Command. [The Prairie Command] should converge
towards Fargo in North Dakota . . . and then continue a
general advance in the direction of Minneapolis and St.
Paul. The occupation of Minneapolis and St. Paul would cut
most of the lines leading to Duluth . . . and would have a
tendency to protect
our railway communications through the Kenora and Rainy
River Districts.
Great Lakes Command. [The Great Lakes Command] will,
generally speaking, remain on the defensive, but rapid and
well organised raids should be made across the Niagara
Frontier, the St. Clair Frontier, the Detroit Frontier and
the St. Mary's Frontier, with sufficient troops to establish
bridgeheads.
Québec Command. [The Québec Command] will take the offensive
on both sides of the Adirondack Mountains with a view of
converging. . . .
in the vicinity of Albany, N.Y.
Maritime Command. [The Maritime Command] will make an
offensive into the State of Maine.

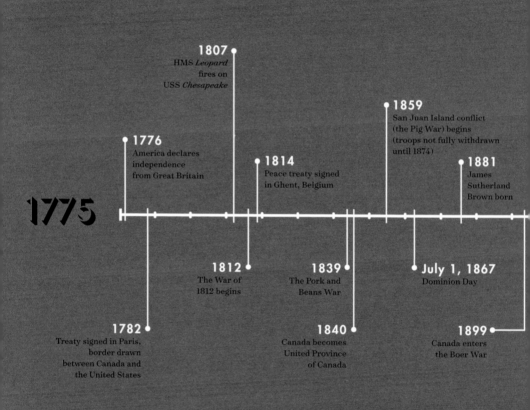

1775

1807
HMS *Leopard* fires on USS *Chesapeake*

1776
America declares independence from Great Britain

1814
Peace treaty signed in Ghent, Belgium

1859
San Juan Island conflict (the Pig War) begins (troops not fully withdrawn until 1874)

1881
James Sutherland Brown born

1812
The War of 1812 begins

1839
The Pork and Beans War

July 1, 1867
Dominion Day

1782
Treaty signed in Paris, border drawn between Canada and the United States

1840
Canada becomes United Province of Canada

1899
Canada enters the Boer War

1935
US-Canada war games held at Fort Drum, New York

1930
War Plan Red written

2005
Independent Task Force on North America, organized by Canada, the United States, and Mexico, urges the creation of a "North American Economic and Security Community."

Security and Prosperity Partnership (SPP) signed by US President George W. Bush, Canadian Prime Minister Paul Martin, and Mexican President Vicente Fox

2011
US President Barack Obama and Canadian Prime Minister Stephen Harper cancel SPP

1938
FDR's address at Queen's University

2012
US President Barack Obama denies plan to invade Canada

1917
The United States enters World War I

1939
Canada enters World War II

2015

1921
Defence Scheme No. 1 written

1957
NORAD formed

2014
US General Martin Dempsey, Chairman of the Joint Chiefs of Staff, denies plan to invade Canada

1941
The United States enters World War II

2002
NORTHCOM formed

1914
Canada enters World War I

2000
Mexican presidential candidate Vicente Fox advocates for the creation of a North American Union, incorporating Mexico, the United States, and Canada into a European Union–style single market

BRITONS
AND
CANADIANS
IN THE U.S.

Show Your
Loyalty to
the Land You
are Living in

ENLIST NOW
IN
BRITISH or CANADIAN AR
AND
Carry Your Flag along side the Stars and S

Acknowledgments

Working on this book as author rather than my usual role as publisher has been an eye-opening, but gratifying, experience. Above all, I've been lucky to work with two excellent editors here: first Jay Sacher, who encouraged a lighter tone to a first draft, then Tom Cho, whose diligent, careful, and patient work improved the book immeasurably and, more important, made it happen. Designer Mia Johnson made it look better than I could've imagined. A hearty thank-you to all three, as well as to my other colleagues at the Press who've encouraged this project. Marielle Suba journeyed to the James Sutherland Brown Archives at Queen's University on my behalf, and Tom Cho and Meredith Baber navigated the labyrinth of the National Archives in Washington, DC, tracking down source documents related to Defence Scheme No. 1 and War Plan Red, respectively.

I am particularly grateful to Jamie Broadhurst of Raincoast Books, who read an early draft and offered numerous excellent suggestions based on his own deep knowledge of Canadian history. Dr. Orest Rudzik, retired University of Toronto, also offered comments and caught several factual errors.

Sources

My quick sketches of the War of 1812 draw heavily on Donald Hickey's *War of 1812: A Forgotten Conflict, Bicentennial Edition* (Urbana: University of Illinois Press, 2012).

The Pig War is the subject of several books, including E. C. Coleman's *The Pig War: The Most Perfect War in History* (Stroud, UK: The History Press, 2009) and Mike Vouri's *The Pig War: Standoff at Griffin Bay* (Seattle: University of Washington Press, 2013).

Britain's role in the Civil War is exhaustively covered in Amanda Foreman's *World on Fire: Britain's Crucial Role in the Civil War* (New York: Random House, 2011), while Canada's surprising involvement in the War Between the States is the subject of John Boyko's *Blood and Daring: How Canada Fought the American Civil War and Forged a Nation* (New York: Knopf, 2013).

Anybody interested in the early history of Canada, and the fascinating man who pieced the country together, should read Richard Gwyn's *Nation Maker: Sir John A. Macdonald: His Life, Our Times* (Mississauga, Ontario: Random House Canada, 2011).

Atholl Sutherland Brown's biography of his father, *Buster: A Canadian Patriot and Imperialist; The Life and Times of Brigadier James Sutherland Brown* (Waterloo, Ontario: Trafford Publishing, 2006), is the best source of information on Buster Brown and Defence Scheme No. 1.

Information on War Plan Red comes primarily from John Major's article "War Plan Red: The American Plan for War with Britain," *Historian 58*, no. 1 (1998): 12–15.

For the most recent thinking on the benefits of a US-Canada "mutual annexation," see Diane Francis's *Merger of the Century: Why Canada of America Should Become One Country* (New York: HarperCollins, 2013).

The most scholarly and in-depth book on this subject is Richard A. Preston's *The Defence of the Undefended Border: Planning for War in North America 1867–1939* (Montreal: McGill-Queen's University Press, 1977).

Floyd W. Rudmin's book *Bordering on Agression: Evidence of US Military Preparations Against Canada* (Québec: Voyageur Publishing, 1993) is the most comprehensive on the subject of War Plan Red.

Credits

The images in this book have been researched and are believed to be in the public domain unless otherwise stated:

p. 13 (Fig. 2)
Courtesy of Marc Ankenbauer

p. 24 (Fig. 7)
Courtesy of Nova Scotia Archives

p. 34 (Fig. 10)
Courtesy of Chippewa Valley Museum

p. 59 (Figs. 22 and 23)
Courtesy of Atholl Sutherland Brown

p. 64 (Fig. 25)
Courtesy of Atholl Sutherland Brown

p. 76 (Fig. 27)
Courtesy of the Franklin D. Roosevelt Presidential Library and Museum, Hyde Park, New York

pp. 86-87 (bottom-right of collage)
Courtesy of Richard Schlecht

pp. 90-121
War Plan Red transcript by F. W. Rudmin, Queen's University, and available online at http://www.glasnost.de/hist/usa/1935invasion.html

pp. 124-32
Defence Scheme No. 1 transcript by Tao Yue, Princeton University, and available online at http://www.taoyue.com/stacks/articles/defence-scheme-one.html?page=0,1

About the Author

Kevin Lippert was born in Leeds, England, but grew up in the United States in Ohio. He studied history and architecture at Princeton University, where he founded Princeton Architectural Press, the publisher of books on architecture, art, design, and visual culture, which he's run for the past thirty-four years. He lives in New York's Hudson Valley with his wife, daughter, and two sons, one of whom is an aspiring writer, and the other an officer cadet in the British Army. His mother is a naturalized Canadian citizen living in Toronto.